RATLINER

H. BACON

HANGAR 1 PUBLISHING

Copyright © 2024 by H. Bacon

All rights reserved.

No part of this book may be reproduced in any form or by any electronic or mechanical means, including information storage and retrieval systems, without written permission from the author, except for the use of brief quotations in a book review.

I dedicate this book to my three children, Daniel, Laura, and Luke, who are brutally honest; to my friends and family, who have been patiently waiting and supportive, providing feedback and suggestions; and to my dog, Molly —sorry, girl, I'll play with you more now.

Special thanks to:

Dr. Greg Bradsher, retired Director of the Holocaust-Era Assets Records Project at the National Archives & Records Administration, for his insight and expertise. Lisa DeLeon, lyricist, who wrote this poem for Ratliner:

> *We seek lost treasure from deep within*
> *And find the secrets of man's dark sin.*
> *Through the dust and stories told*
> *A lifetime of secrets start to unfold.*

Special thanks to my editor, Shelly Mascia of Shelley's Editing Service, and my publisher, Hangar 1 Publishing, for their belief in me, support, and patience.

CONTENTS

1. Bratislava	1
2. The Head Office of the SS	3
3. Kansas City	4
4. Austria	38
5. Marriott Hotel	54
6. London	67
7. New York City	69
8. Austria	78
9. Washington, DC - Holocaust Museum	122
10. Kansas City	131
11. Brussels	132
12. London	133
13. Brooklyn	134
14. Chicago	135
15. Kansas City	137
16. Independence	138
About the Author	143
Afterword	145

1

BRATISLAVA

1939

The chattering birds in the tree-lined avenue suddenly became silent. The stillness was broken by a gentle breeze that caused the leaves on the sidewalk to spiral up into a tiny whirlwind. A single leaf, caught in the airstream was forced up the landscaped walk, into the gated yard, up the stone steps to the massive oak door that suddenly flew open with a bang, causing the birds to take flight with a chaotic cackling.

"*Aus! Jetzt!*" ("Out! Now!") The burly Schutstaffel officer shoved the family out of their home, crushing the leaf underfoot, into the street to join the growing stream of people being pushed and jostled toward the edge of town, into the woods.

Young Daniel stole one last look over his shoulder at his home before it disappeared. His sister, Becky, and brothers, Nathan and Joseph, were already lost in the crowd. The memory was burned into his mind: an SS soldier standing on the stoop, nonplussed, noting in a journal the items being taken out of his family's estate. Daniel caught one last glimpse of a cherished painting that had been in their family for generations being taken out of their home and carefully set in the truck that had pulled up in front of the walk. A sudden sharp blow sent shafts of pain searing through his shoulder as the gun butt prodded him forward.

"*Schnell!*" Confusion and fear ruled the crowd. The street, which had been barren moments before, was now crowded with star-emblazoned residents — families, old women, small children; each laden with whatever valuables they could carry and food for the trip to regions unknown. Daniel had a sinking feeling that he may never see his home again as he stumbled forward in a stupor, melding into the crowd like cattle to the yards, a low murmur of prayers and soft sobs breaking the silence.

The SS trooper assigned to the estate continued to inventory the items taken from the home. He prided himself in his ability to provide meticulous records to his superior and, in the process, block out any responsibility for what he really knew about what would happen to the sea of citizens pouring out into the streets. He kept reminding himself that he was only following orders, but eventually, months later, after all his forced "following orders," he'd silence his conscience by taking his own life. He finalized his notes, snapped the ledger shut, and moved to the next home.

2

THE HEAD OFFICE OF THE SS

Reinhard Heydrich whistled when he saw the painting. "Excellent. A Vermeer." Although Hitler himself would appreciate this old master's work, Heydrich thought he deserved his own private collection. This painting of the girl would be a nice addition. He packed up the painting and hid it at the back of his closet and returned to the young officer in the front office.

"These are complete," the junior SS officer said while handing Heydrich the journals.

As Stellvertretender Reichsprotektor in the Protectorate of Bohemia and Moravia, Reinhard Heydrich oversaw all records, which he kept carefully stored in his office. Heydrich added the volumes to the collection — an unending supply of similar ledgers, each stored precisely in marked boxes, true to his penchant for detail — a mark of the Reich. Heydrich was tall and attractive, a favorite among the ladies, but his shark-like eyes were cold; lifeless and blue.

3

KANSAS CITY
PRESENT DAY

"Yes, I have it." The shark-blue eyes of the grizzled old man flared as he breathlessly barked into the phone with a stiff German clip. "No, he is gone. The only other one left is slowly being eaten alive by cancer. He can't talk anymore. They've put a tracheotomy in his neck, and the Parkinson's is not letting him write anything. Don't worry, it's taken care of. Trust me, he'll be out of pain soon."

The elder version of the man, still an imposing figure, didn't have the patience to be spoken to like a child by the person on the other end of the phone. He could still do everything he'd always been able to, even though others thought differently, especially concerning his independence. He still insisted on driving himself, for instance. They had wanted him to have a driver, but he refused; like many octogenarians, he still believed he was a safe driver. His deteriorating body betrayed his mental capacity, which frustrated him. As much as those around him doubted his ability, no one could stop him from doing what he wished. He had been homeward bound when the call came in and pulled sharply to the side of the road. He had passed on the information that they had needed and now was anxious to resume his journey.

"Fine, fine, you'll be pleased with him. Goodbye." He hung up. "Bastard."

Now I can get out of here, he thought, his blood pressure still soaring as he accelerated to merge back into the interstate traffic from the shoulder.

Blasted cars. Get out of my way!

He quickly pulled back into traffic, blissfully unaware of the monstrous, double semi-truck barreling around the curve behind him, bearing down on his vehicle.

The semi plowed into the black Mercedes in slow motion, sending it spinning, showering the road and surrounding terrain in bits of the car that moments before had held the cursing Henry Conrad.

* * *

"This is Jessica. How may I help you?" The call began like a multitude of others, typical of any other real estate conversation, this time regarding the listing of an inherited home to settle an estate. "Sure, when does your plane arrive? Okay, I'll meet you at the house."

Jessica Sinclair, a multi-million-dollar realtor, jotted down the address and began to compile information regarding the home that her new client wished her to sell. As much as she loved interacting with her clients, research was her favorite thing. Knowledge is power, and the more informed she was, the more confidence she exuded.

The county's records indicated the home was a stately residence in a grand old neighborhood with sizable yards and mature trees. She knew the house and had admired it for years. It was a beautiful stone and brick mansion behind elegant brick and wrought iron gates. It was a much easier job to sell a home she would love to own herself.

From the comparable sales she pulled, it looked like the home would sell for over a million. That kind of commission sure would come in handy. The economy had wreaked havoc on her income, and she was eager for the tide to turn.

It didn't take Jessica long to assemble an impressive listing packet for her new client. By the appointment time, Jessica was excited to meet her newest prospect.

* * *

"Hi. You must be Karl Conrad," Jessica said as she shook Karl's hand, flashing her winning smile, her gaze reaching up to the heights of his face. He was tall and blonde with clear blue eyes that drew her in and wouldn't let go. She took an involuntary intake of breath.

"Hello. Yes, I'm Karl. And you must be Jessica. Glad you could meet me here on such short notice," he said with a dazzling grin.

Jessica had to pull herself away from those eyes. Mentally kicking herself for not looking away sooner, she said, "No problem. I was happy to help you out. I've always thought this home was awesome, and I'm thrilled to be able to see what's inside."

"Great. Well, then come on in, and let me show you around. I've disabled the security system, so it's safe," Karl said, sweeping his hand downward to indicate the ankle-high infrared sensors in the walls.

"I haven't been here for ages. My parents didn't see eye to eye about most things with my grandfather, and after they passed away, well, I just never came back," Karl explained as he escorted Jessica down the hall. "Maybe I should have, but I wasn't close to him by that time."

Jessica was not disappointed. The grandeur of the interior exceeded her imagination. They went from room to room, Jessica taking notes about the home's attributes, the rooms' dimensions, and snapping photographs.

The living room was adorned with magnificent paintings hung in ornate gilded frames. The leather furniture was massive and with strategically placed statues and marble busts. It reeked of old money.

"Impressive." Jessica whistled. "Your Grandpa Conrad had good taste."

"Runs in the family." Karl laughed. "At least I know where I get it. Too bad I can't fit it all in my place in Chicago. I'll have to get rid of most of this stuff."

The living room had pocket doors that opened into the library. All four walls were lined floor to ceiling with leather-bound volumes. In the center of the room was a circular mahogany table, with a chess set left in the middle of a strategic move.

"Wow... There's so much that will need to be inventoried. Someone's got their work cut out for them. This is going to be quite a chore for you to organize and sell, isn't it?" Jessica mused.

"Well..." Karl said hesitantly, "That's something else I wanted to discuss with you. As you can see, the house is full, and I have no idea what value everything has. Plus, I only planned to be away from my office for a short while — not nearly enough time to figure out what to do with it all. Since I have no idea who to trust or hire to help me here in Kansas City..." He stopped in the dining room across the table from Jessica and turned to face her. "How about you?"

He had to be well over six feet tall, early forties; bronzed complexion with an air about him that indicated he was used to getting what he wanted just by flashing his perfect smile and turning on the charm. Jessica was enjoying working with him already. Being tied to him indefinitely by the sale of the household goods wouldn't ordinarily be something she'd consider.

"Oh... Uh, okay," Jessica replied. She thought, the wheels already turning, *I don't usually deal with the belongings of a home, just the selling of the house itself, but I used to have an antique store, and I do know someone who is experienced with estate sales...*

"Great." Karl, pleased, slammed both hands down on the dining room table, making Jessica jump. "I was hoping you would. Now, let's continue our tour."

Karl confidently led the way into the next room. Jessica stepped aside to follow him, watching his muscular body undulate through his thin business shirt, as she was escorted through the house.

What have you done? Jessica chastised herself, knowing that agreeing to assist him came from ulterior motives. *Would you have honestly agreed to do this if he wasn't so attractive?*

She suspected he made a habit of using his charm and good looks to get anything he wanted. Since she was single, Jessica automatically stared at his ringless left hand and wondered if he was available.

Get a grip — you're not thinking with your head anymore, girl. And besides, he's probably taken. All the good ones are. With my luck, he probably doesn't even like women. Got to keep focused. Straighten up!

They completed their tour of the main level. Karl followed Jessica up the stairs to the next level as more quality paintings and embellishments came into view.

Jessica's long, dark locks bounced as she ascended, her toned calves taking the steps with ease. Karl lightly touched her elbow as they reached the top of the stairway, nudging her to one side.

"This was Grandpa's bedroom."

The room had a Medieval air, as if they had stepped back in time. The massive bed had carvings straight from the Black Forest snaking up the four posts. Matching dressers lined the walls and sensual paintings and gilded mirrors were everywhere. She coughed lightly at the smell; a combination of old man, cigar, cologne, and soiled socks.

"Uh, yeah... His room always kind of creeped me out," Karl confessed.

"I can see why," Jessica replied, snapping a couple of photos. "I'm ready to move to the next room if you are," she said, not wanting to dwell on what may have happened there.

The other bedrooms were standard guest rooms, filled with beds, dressers, and overstuffed chairs. The last room they entered, at the end of the long hallway, was a gentleman's parlor; a den reminiscent of a smoking room where men would gather and drink brandy. The heavy stale air encouraged them to move on.

"Is there an attic? I thought I saw a small window from the outside," Jessica asked as they finished the tour, poking her head in the closets, looking for an attic access.

"Well, there must be, but I've never been in it. Can't see where you'd get into it, though," Karl said, also looking around. After an unsuccessful few minutes, they gave up and headed downstairs.

"Basement?" Jessica inquired.

"*That* I can find," Karl said as he led Jessica through the kitchen.

"Hm, the kitchen needs updating. That will count against you when we market this. But it's cool that there's a dumbwaiter," Jessica noted.

"Well, the updating thing can't be helped. It's not worth it for me to put any money into this place. Whoever buys it will need to take it as-is," Karl said as they wound past the work center to the basement door.

The dark, dank old cellar held a few old wine bottles and canning jars filled with beets and watermelon pickles, covered with dust, all lined up perfectly. Old boxes filled another shelf, while tools all stored in descending order by size were lined up above an old workbench, the ceiling dripping with ancient cobwebs.

"Ick. I've seen enough," Jessica said, turning abruptly to go back up the stairs, a cold shiver running up her spine as she brushed imaginary cobwebs off her shoulders, muttering, "I *hate* spiders."

As Karl and Jessica creaked up the stairs toward the daylight, they were unaware that deep in the dark recesses, behind a tall cabinet, hid a door. One that hadn't been opened in a very, very long time.

* * *

"Well, it looks like I've got my work cut out for me," Jessica said as she pulled several papers out of her briefcase. They were back in the drawing room. "I'll get right on it once we get this paperwork signed."

The necessary business complete, Karl handed the papers back to Jessica, then gave her a keyring packed with keys. "I have no idea which key goes to what, except this one is for the front door. So, I'm giving them all to you, there. Good luck."

"Thanks... I think," she said with an air of disappointment over the heavy task before her.

"Listen, I'm sorry to meet and run like this, but I've got to catch my plane, and I still have some business to take care of. Are we good? If you need anything, you have all my contact information." Karl was gathering up his papers as he headed toward the door, stopping midway to face Jessica. "I feel a whole lot better now that I can leave this in your hands."

I bet, Jessica thought, then said with a smile, "Don't worry about a thing."

"Keep me posted," Karl said as he shook Jessica's hand, noticing how petite her soft, warm hand was in his. He reluctantly let go and headed out the door. He felt bad leaving Jessica with all the work, but he still needed to get to the bank before catching his flight.

* * *

Karl, the only surviving family member, was notified of his grandfather's death by phone from the first police officer to arrive at the scene of the accident. He met Karl at the airport as soon as Karl had exited the plane.

"He seemed very angry that he was obviously going to die," the officer had told him, "but insisted that I find you personally and give you this." The officer handed Karl a small envelope that had his name and address on the outside. "It was in his wallet. It's in here with all his personal things. Now, if you could just sign this paper for me…"

Karl signed and was handed the packet. It felt odd to have his grandfather's effects handed to him in one large brown envelope, as if his life was condensed to this hodgepodge collection of personal items.

"I know he was your grandpa, and I'm sorry for your loss, and if he hadn't been dying, well, frankly, I wouldn't have done this. I'm sure you meant a lot to him by the way he carried on about you," he said as he shook Karl's hand. "Well, thanks. Gotta head out."

The officer had almost refused to honor the last request based solely on the dying man's condescending attitude. He owed him no favors for what he had called him or the disrespect he'd given the emergency crew, the ones attempting to save his life. He forgave him, though, primarily because he was, after all, dying, and who knew how anyone would behave in the last moments of one's life? One thing was for sure — it couldn't be any worse than Henry Conrad's last moments.

* * *

Karl had felt nothing at the news of his grandfather's passing. It bothered him. He could have rationalized the lack of emotion over the loss of the only remaining family member by reminding himself that he didn't even really know him. Even so, just an inkling of remorse would have comforted him. Instead, he approached the death and settling of his grandfather's estate like any other business deal he handled; go in, assess the situation, and get it done.

Karl hardly remembered his Grandpa Conrad. Only a few somber childhood memories came to him: sunlight streaming through the paned library windows, hazy with smoke wafting from the deer's head Meerschaum pipe; his grandpa, feet propped up on the upholstered footstool, hidden behind the newspaper he was reading; or his gruff voice, heavy with his native German accent — "Your turn, boy." — as Karl took a whooping in chess.

Most of the memories were harsh, hateful words, cutting deep as Karl's father fought with his papa about every subject imaginable. Father and son were opposites politically, religiously, emotionally, even physically. Grandpa Conrad had been tall at one time — now several inches shorter due to age, but still taller than Karl's father, Vincent. Vincent, or Vinny, had been a football player with a kind, gentle demeanor who was just as stout and muscular as his father was tall and lean. He preferred equal rights over "might makes right."

Grandpa Karl was never one to be politically correct on any issue, but he was fair. He despised all others with equal disdain, something Vinny had no patience for. Vinny became a civil rights activist in college, found his true love in the sixties, married young, and produced a love child, whom they named Karl.

After Karl was born, Grandpa Conrad took a keen interest in the beautiful "golden child" and insisted Karl visit him on a regular basis.

Mein Reinrassig was Grandpa's nickname for him, whatever that meant.

Karl didn't spend much time with his grandfather during high school or college. When the job opportunity arose in Chicago, he took it and never looked back. His grandfather had kept trying to draw him back home, but it just didn't appeal to Karl.

His disenchantment with his grandfather began about ten years ago when Karl heard of his parents' fatal accident. After his grandfather didn't even attend the funeral, Karl cut him off. Their relationship was never renewed, despite several attempts from his grandfather, the most recent one just a few weeks ago. As far as Karl was concerned, his grandfather had been dead to him for years.

* * *

As he drove, Karl reviewed the list in his mind. *Funeral... Check. House... Check. Bank... Next on the agenda.* On the small envelope the police officer had given him from his grandfather was written *Henry Conrad, Nations Bank, 2074 Ward Parkway, Kansas City, MO Account #53902876*.

Nations Bank took up an entire city block and, from the architectural style, dated to the mid-twentieth century. Karl parked across the street. The huge doors of the intimidating structure opened silently at his approach. The lobby was unusually silent for such a large repository, his footsteps echoing forty feet above to the vaulted ceiling. Karl made a beeline for the clerk behind the reception desk at the center of the room.

According to the directions in the envelope, Karl requested to speak to a Mr. Berg. His words were absorbed into the hushed atmosphere. He felt like a little boy called into the principal's office.

"One moment, sir," the clerk said as she walked briskly to a private office, returning immediately. "Right this way, Mr. Conrad," she said as she led him down the long hallway.

Did I tell her my name? Karl wondered but dismissed the thought as they continued past the public elevators. She stopped in front of one marked *Private: Authorized Personnel Only* and entered a six-digit code into the security keypad. The doors opened.

"The elevator will take you to Mr. Berg's office," she told him and returned to her desk as he entered the posh lift. Karl took in the grandeur of the space — dark paneling, gilded mirrors, mother of pearl inlay on the buttons — as he rose silently to the top floor. The doors opened, and Karl stepped out into a lavish corporate office suite that encompassed the entire top floor of the bank building.

A leggy blonde supermodel-secretary greeted him with an inviting smile. "Thank you for coming, Mr. Conrad. This way, please."

This time, he knew for a fact that he had not introduced himself. She delivered him to an office emblazoned with *James Berg, Esq.* on the door.

"Mr. Conrad is here," she announced, opening the door to reveal a shriveled man behind a massive desk.

"Hello, Mr. Conrad. So pleased to meet you." Mr. Berg greeted him with a toothy smile as he warmly pumped his hand.

Did he just click his heels? Karl thought. "Hello," he said hesitantly. "I don't understand."

"Yes, of course. My apologies. You must not have known, and I'm sure your grandfather, a wonderful man, God rest his soul, knew you would make this trip one day. He was a special client, your grandfather. Did I mention that I admired him very much?"

Geez, thought Karl, *what is up with this guy?*

To Mr. Berg, Karl replied, "Oh, well, that's great. Nice to meet you, too."

"Here, follow me," Mr. Berg said. "I'm sure his safety deposit box will be of interest to you."

"Okay, sure."

Mr. Berg took Karl to a vault room, accessed through two large, secure steel doors, to a room full of thousands of safety deposit boxes. At the rear of the room was another vault door that led into a small room, also lined with boxes.

"Let's see... Yes... here we are. One, zero, zero, nine. Your grandfather's box. Do you have your key?"

Karl handed him the key from the envelope. Mr. Berg slid both keys into their slots, opened the door, pulled the long box out, and set it on a table in the private room in the vault.

"I will leave you now. Please ring that bell when you are ready to leave." Mr. Berg exited through a side door that locked behind him.

Karl sat, frozen for a few moments, absorbing the enormity of what could be stored in such a secure place. It could be anything. People stored their most cherished possessions in safety deposit boxes; that encouraged Karl's imagination to run rampant as he slowly opened it, unsure of its contents. Would it be jewels? Or gold?

Only one way to find out. Karl took a deep breath and slowly opened the lid. He exhaled in disappointment. All he saw was a stack of papers and a couple more keys.

Another disappointment, Grandpa. Way to go. Thanks a lot.

He immediately chastised himself for his thoughts leaning toward greed when he should have, in fact, been grieving. Humbled, Karl pocketed the contents, stood, and rang the bell.

* * *

From his office window, Mr. Berg watched Karl's figure far below exit the building and cross the street to his car. The old man picked up the phone and hit speed dial. "He's been here," Mr. Berg said and hung up the receiver.

* * *

"Honey, I'm home," Karl yelled as he re-entered his grandfather's home. "Hey, I'm back. Miss me?" He breezed through the first floor, finally finding Jessica attempting to match keys to doors.

"Oh, you're back. Long time no see. Just couldn't stay away, could you?" Jessica said, straightening from a crouch.

"Listen, I ran over to the bank, and there were a few more keys there, so here ya go. Have fun. Hate to pop in like this and go again, but I've gotta run to catch my flight back to Chicago. Call me if you need me." And as quickly as he arrived, Karl was gone.

Jessica watched Karl jump into his rental car and speed off toward the airport. "Bye," Jessica quietly said as she gave a little wave before closing the door, the car already out of view.

Jessica looked at the new keys that Karl had deposited in her hand. There were several old ones, about the right age of the house. She added them to her keyring and kept on trying to match the keys to the locks.

* * *

After Karl initially left, Jessica had placed a call to her long-time friend, Kathy Malz. Kathy ran an estate sale business, a long-time associate from Jessica's antique store days. Their business association had created a mutual respect which had resulted in a long-lasting friendship. Kathy should have been arriving at any moment, which made Jessica feel a bit less creeped out by the empty house.

I wonder why old people like to block out all the daylight with heavy curtains. Jessica assessed the room, her eyes drawn to the velvet drapes. *Those will have to go to let some natural light in here.* She pulled down the old, upholstered curtains.

The transformation was immediate. The room glowed with a golden hue, which encouraged Jessica to go room to room removing all the window coverings.

Sheers would be awesome here. Diffused light would be perfect.

The old familiar feeling of accomplishment enveloped Jessica. There was something comforting about transforming a space from gloom to glorious. Staging homes to be more presentable for sale was her forte.

The doorbell rang. Kathy had arrived. Jessica greeted her warmly and showed her around, glad to have another living soul in the house.

"Let me know if you need anything. I'll be upstairs. It's amazing what a difference it makes when you let the sunshine in," Jessica said as she climbed the stairs and made her way from room to room. As she visited each room, she straightened crooked pictures and adjusted displays to create a better composition.

"There. Done," she said as she took the final drapes down in the upstairs library.

As she perused the room with a critical eye, admiring the transformation from dark to light, Jessica noticed an unnatural shadow along the bookcase.

That just doesn't make sense, she thought, crossing the room to examine it closer.

The bookcase wasn't flush against the wall; one side was about half an inch from the wall and the other flat against it. She was about to push the bookcase back in place when she felt a draft from behind the bookcase.

"Jessica..." A breathy voice was barely heard across the slight breeze.

She turned at the sound. *Did I really just hear that?*

A chill ran up her back, raising the hair on her arms and back of her neck. Finding no one in the room, Jessica shook off her fear, rationalizing the sound away as just her imagination combined with the eeriness of the house.

She took a deep breath and turned back to the bookcase. Jessica ran her fingers along the gap and realized it was not a solid wall behind the bookcase, but an opening. She slid her fingers in all the way and pulled. The bookcase swung silently on a pivot hinge, opening like a door to reveal a dark corridor. Steps rose and disappeared into the darkness.

Although every fiber of her being screamed "Run! Don't do it." She couldn't help herself. Her curiosity was too strong, and the pull from above was something she couldn't fight. She slowly ascended the steps.

At the top of the stairs was an old dusty door, barely illuminated by the light from the library streaming through the opening. Jessica hesitantly reached for the doorknob and slowly turned the handle as her heart pounded so hard, she could hardly breathe.

Locked.

Quickly she went through the assortment of keys, none fitting, until she tried one of the few Karl had just given her. There was a *click*, and she turned the doorknob.

The door slowly opened with a drawn-out *creak*.

She'd found the attic.

But why the secret bookcase and the locked door?

She surveyed the long, dark space. The window she'd seen from the outside was in the distance, at the end of the eave. Finding the light switch, she flipped it on.

All that was in the attic were several trunks and a bunch of boxes. It was large enough to finish out another couple of rooms — she noted to herself to mention that to potential buyers. She let herself breathe. *Nothing to be afraid of here.*

The trunks had obviously been there a long time, if the accumulated dust was any indication. They were metal, reminiscent of a military type of issue. The boxes seemed a more recent addition — white computer boxes, no dust gathered, and a path cut through the dirty floor where they had been slid across the room. She was about to turn around and leave the attic but hesitated, realizing that there may be something to include in the estate sale stored within the trunks and boxes.

Jessica went to the first trunk and tried to open it, but it was locked.

Hm... Looks like I need a key. Good thing I have a bazillion of them.

"Score," she said out loud, using one of the other keys Karl gave her.

There was a click as the latch popped open. Inside was a variety of items — photos, books, clothing — all layered with dust. From the photos, it was WWII-era; obviously Karl's grandpa, Henry Conrad. Karl was a spitting image of his grandpa.

From watching years of the *Antiques Road Show*, she knew WWII memorabilia commanded top dollar. Jessica gingerly lifted the uniform out of its shrine. The dusty cloth made her cough.

Very cool. Jessica whistled. *...What's this? Wait a second.*

Jessica caught her breath at the emblem on the sleeve. A swastika. She dropped the uniform and started rifling through the photos. She saw ancient photos of what must have been Henry Conrad, too identical to Karl to be anyone else, with other soldiers, with Hitler, with other men, those she didn't know but were obviously important from their uniforms — all wearing the crazy spider leg swastika on their arms. Karl's grandfather was a Nazi.

Jessica's stomach knotted. On the back of the photos, each person was noted in precise penmanship — Hitler, Himmler, Goering, Goebbels — but not once did she see Henry Conrad's name. Instead, she read *Reinhard Heydrich* on every photo of Karl's grandpa.

Jessica went to the next trunk. Inside were handwritten journals, ledgers, and records. On the cover of each book read *Auschwitz*, *Birkenau*, or *Buchenwald*, penned in a beautiful script. She opened one of them. In it, she read names, dates, items collected — thousands of entries. She grabbed ledger after ledger; more of the same. Dropping the book, she vomited.

Horrified, Jessica ran from one box to another — tearing open the lids to uncover hundreds of similar ledgers. *Dachau, Belzec, Majdanek, Sobibor, Treblinka, Merkers MIne, Reichsbank, Berlin, Hamburg, Prague*. It was a comprehensive inventory of valuables taken from Jews as well as other "undesirables" across Europe. This collection of ledgers was a death list.

The seatbelt sign had just been turned off. Karl reached under the seat in front of him, maneuvered his stowed item onto his lap, opened his briefcase, and removed the packet of papers from his grandfather's safety deposit box.

Might as well see what we've got here, Karl thought as he opened the packet on his tray table. On the top of the pile was a letter addressed to him.

My Reinrassig Karl, (typical Grandpa, again with the weird nickname)

If you are reading this, something must have happened to me, and I am dead.

A slow chill began crawling up Karl's spine.

It is time you know the truth. I never trusted your father enough to bring him into 'The Circle', but you, Karl, are exceptional. Ever since you were a child, I knew you'd be the one to trust. It is of the utmost importance that you keep secret — for your own protection — what I am going to reveal to you. Others don't agree with me. They think you are not pure enough to share what I'm about to tell you, but you and I are much alike.

I've known that from the first day your damn hippy parents brought you to me.

Know this, my Liebchen, you redeemed your father in my eyes. He was a complete disappointment to me.

Karl's deep-seated anger began to bristle.

He was so lost — never a true son to me. But he was still my flesh and blood. I'm sorry, that must sound confusing, but I know you will soon understand. I know you have hated me for not attending your parents' funeral, but now I must tell you, I was there. I had to be. He was my son. As hard as it is for you to understand, I did love him; he was of my blood, no matter what stupid things he did.

I could not be seen, because my enemies were also there. But others were there, too — those who want to protect you and will help perfect you as a part of the Inner Circle. You have been chosen and trained—

Huh? Karl thought. *Trained?*

—for a much larger destiny than you could ever have imagined.

Karl's emotions welled with a renewed hatred he had harbored for his grandfather. Much of his personal problems over the years were rooted in his dysfunctional upbringing.

Karl thought of himself as a toddler playing with his grandpa; laughing, happy — chubby angel with golden curls loving his grandpapa. The memories submerged in his subconscious began to surface; fun, loving times together at first, then snippets of darker memories.

"Isn't that lovely?" His grandpa would say, pointing out specific images in the children's books he read to Karl. But anything without the idyllic WASPish image would be "Look how ugly — that's disgusting."

The memories flooded back, Grandpa teaching him to fence with a tipped sword or play the violin, rapping his hand sharply for any errors; the uniform Grandpa gave him, the marching, his toy gun complete with bayonet jabbing the teddy bears and making the stuffing fly with a gleeful laugh. Even in the garden — planting the seeds, waiting for the plants to grow, and then eliminating the weak seedlings so the strong ones could have more room to grow.

"It is the only way the strong will thrive," Grandpa had said. "You must sacrifice the weak to make room for the others."

* * *

"What would you like to drink?"

Karl, immersed in the letter, jumped as the flight attendant jolted him back to reality. He was sweating. Karl adjusted the air vents as he decided not to order his usual beverage.

"Whiskey, please, and a glass of ice water," he told her and went back to the letter.

* * *

...Remember our chess games? Life is a chess game, Karl. You must plan your every move; anticipate your opponent's next move, then the next one, then the next, having a plan to respond to each move that is made. Never underestimate your opponent — that is crucial. You can never let your king be taken! You are the king, but there are others who will try to take you. Do not be afraid. You have the skills that I taught you. You, as I have been, will be superior.

Now I need to tell you my secret, and unless my instincts about you are wrong, you will be proud of your grandpa and ready to continue protecting my — rather, our — past. Remember the photos of the great men I used to show you in the uniforms?

Karl found himself nodding, vaguely remembering soldiers, lots of soldiers, with his grandpa among them.

They were my associates; my friends, my peers. I was in their secret circle and chosen to be trusted with information that only three of us officers were allowed to guard. We were given new identities and sent around the world to live where no one knew us.

My grandson, I am so proud to finally reveal to you your heritage. Your father never knew. He rejected me and my teachings early in his life and was worthless, so he did not deserve to know. I cannot tell you how proud I was of you, my sonnenkinder.

Every disappointment from your father was forgiven when he gave you to me for those brief times we had together. I only wish that you had not rejected me after your parents died. But I knew our years together would never be forgotten.

Karl stopped reading and thought back to the man he was ten years ago; arrogant, filled with hate, a true bigot who thought too much of himself. He was the best at whatever he attempted. Unabashed success breeds superiority. He could do no wrong and thought he knew it all and could have any woman he chose.

Until he met Rachel. He first saw her at the Chicago building where his business leased an office. They entered the ground floor elevator at the same time, and each pressed the button for the seventh floor. She cast him a coy smile, and for him, it was all over. He fell hard. They began "coincidently" taking breaks at the same time, and eventually lunch.

He had worked into it slowly, making sure there was a mutual interest prior to asking her out on a date. Karl was surprised to realize that he didn't know if he would be successful. He was deathly afraid she wouldn't say yes. For the first-time, insecurity entered his life. He did not like that sensation and resolved to, once again, go after and get what he wanted. Relief flooded over him when she said yes when he finally asked her out.

At first, it didn't matter to him what they did or who they associated with as long as he was with her. But eventually Karl became hesitant.

Rachel was a beauty — perfect pale skin and thick blonde hair that always caught the sunlight. Her smoky grey eyes were enchanting. She had a quick, genuine smile, and loved sports. Rachel's petite frame gave her a seemingly delicate stature, but she was tough. Having grown up sparring and checking with her hockey-playing brothers, she was a force to be reckoned with.

She intrigued Karl. At first, their dates were dinner or a movie, shows, and sports events. It progressed to where a visit to meet her family became appropriate. That was the Thanksgiving from hell. They arrived late; the rest of the family had already gathered around the table. Her family, loud, fun, and forgiving, didn't berate them for their tardiness but was just glad to see they were there. An easy-going group — not at all like Karl's family.

"Hey, look who's here. Come on in." The family, en masse, left the dinner table, enveloping Rachel in a warm group hug. Gradually, they noticed Karl and all attention turned to Rachel's guest, who was greeted with strong handshakes and hearty pats to the back.

"Welcome. Let's get an extra chair for Rachel's man," her father said with a wink.

Anyone else would have felt welcomed to the family immediately, but Karl was uncomfortable. Mostly because Rachel's family was a diverse racial mix. There had to be every nationality represented here, and he felt oddly out of place. His disdain was evident, even though he tried to mask it for Rachel's sake. His eyes betrayed his forced politeness, and the few disparaging comments that slipped out were not well received.

Rachel was disappointed. She spent the next few months trying to balance her desire to improve Karl's standing with her family with her personal misgivings about his behavior. As a result, no future family gatherings were on the agenda.

It was the beginning of the end for Rachel. Family was of utmost importance to her, and Karl's inability to accept her family's own personal melting pot was too much for her. Even though Karl told her he loved her despite her family, it wasn't enough for Rachel.

"*Despite* my family? Are you serious? Listen, mister, you love me, you love my family. Period." It was over.

Karl analyzed their failed relationship, comparing Rachel's family to his own. Karl's parents were products of the sixties — free love, no boundaries — which was too loose and fancy-free for Karl. Even when his parents' friends weren't high, they mostly laid around the house without ambition, not accomplishing much of anything. Karl loved his parents, but their lifestyle repulsed him. It caused him to embrace the rigid, no-nonsense, regulated life, and the views of Grandpa Conrad.

It took a couple of years for Karl to sort through his ideology and realize that maybe he didn't, after all, know everything. It finally broke through when he was assigned to work with James. Karl assumed that James had been hired only to fulfill the company's policy for racial diversity. However, Karl was soon humbled and impressed by him.

James was brilliant; he had more degrees, more experience, more panache. The day Karl realized that James was more intelligent than he was, everything changed. Karl had to concede that he admired James, realizing he no longer even noticed the tonal differences of their skin. This revelation rocked Karl's world, and he re-evaluated everything he had known to be true.

By the time Karl's heart softened and was ready to accept all of Rachel's family as his own, it was too late. Rachel had moved on, marrying someone else, gone forever.

Karl hung the closed sign on his heart and threw himself into work. He forced himself to reflect on his upbringing. He realized some of the "lazy" friends of his parents were homeless or downtrodden people that his parents were trying to help. Karl's parents had accepted everyone and anyone into their home who needed love, a good meal, or a roof over their head.

Karl took a hard look at what he had thought to be good times with his grandfather. Upon examination, Grandpa Conrad's ways were too condescending and harsh, even hateful, to anyone who didn't measure up to the high standards Karl thought were his guide for life.

Karl made a decision to treat others not only like he wished to be treated, but better. Karl's cold, hard knot of superiority that had been firmly planted in his heart slowly melted away. In his quest for a humbler outlook, Karl started volunteering at the local homeless shelter and donated large amounts of cash and unwanted items to charity. Even though he didn't appear to be more than a lovelorn workaholic, every day, Karl's goal became to make someone else's day great in some way. Amazingly, this made him content. And the Karl that Grandpa Conrad knew no longer existed.

* * *

The flight attendant brought the drink and handed him a tiny bag of peanuts.

"I heard they actually used to serve a meal on a flight," Karl told the oblivious adolescent sitting next to him nodding to the music blaring from his headset. It took Karl about half a second to consume the airline's fare and get back to his reading.

Of the three of us who started out, I am the only one remaining — or the last to die. One of my comrades succumbed to Alzheimer's, the other to cancer. I was the only remaining keeper of the books. It has been a divine honor to have served our Holy Father and the Reich all my life, and I am entrusting you to continue in my stead. Now, a word of caution: there are those out there who disagree with me and do not believe you are the one to trust with this honor. But you have proven it to me as a child, and I've seen it with your rise to power in the business world. I've always known you would be the one. I, and now you, have the great honor bestowed by Adolf Hitler himself to protect and preserve the records of the Third Reich. In the library upstairs, there is a secret entrance to the attic behind a bookcase. It is there that I have kept the information safe.

My real name is not Henry Karl Conrad. It is Reinhard Tristan Eugen Heydrich. I was third in command for our beloved furor's army. I am sorry to not be able to tell you in person. I would have loved more than anything else to tell you this and see the pride in our true heritage. You are a prince in the Holy Roman Empire, and I am proud to bestow this honor to you. Everything else you need to know is in the house.

Secrecy is paramount. No one must know of this. I trust you, my child. Soon, others will contact you, and you will have their support and protection. There are keys in this safety deposit box that open the trunks. Do not let them out of your sight.

Karl's heart was pounding. Sweat beads glistened on his forehead. He reached up and cranked the air vent open full blast.

"Are you okay?" the passing flight attendant asked. "Can I bring you anything?"

"Uh, I'm fine— Yes, water please."

"Shit," Karl said out loud, and the teenager's mother cast him a dirty look, though her son was still unaware of anything other than the tunes in his headset.

Jessica's in the house, he thought in a panic. *I've got to get back there.*

When the attendant delivered the water, Karl asked, "When is the next flight back to Kansas City?"

"Uh, sir, we just left there," she replied.

"I know, I know. I just realized I need to go back."

* * *

Jessica stumbled down the stairs and made sure the bookcase was pushed tightly against the wall. She got the impression her discovery should not be discussed with Kathy.

I've got to tell Karl, she thought and dialed him, only to get his voicemail. "Hey, it's Jessica, call me. It's really important." Her trembling voice would surely make Karl call back quickly.

Kathy was just finishing her work as Jessica got to the first floor. "Hey, Jessica, got a minute?"

"I'll be right there," Jessica replied. "I just need to run to the bathroom first."

She locked herself in the small room, splashing water in her face and swishing cool water in her mouth to eliminate the vomit aftertaste. She smoothed her hair, put on some fresh lip gloss, and told herself to "man up."

"Okay, you can do this," she muttered as she headed in Kathy's direction.

"Hey, I'm pretty impressed," Kathy told Jessica when they met in the living room. "Usually, I see some kind of eclectic mix of valuables and junk, but this place is quality all the way. I've never seen better reproductions of the old masters than on these walls here. I think your Mr. Conrad will be pleased with the results of the auction."

Jessica realized the artwork might very well be originals.

There's no way Karl had a clue about this. If he did, he would have never left all this in my hands, she thought, then spoke to her friend with forced normalcy.

"Well, Kathy, why don't you give me your preliminary evaluation, and I'll pass it along to Mr. Conrad. I'll let you know when he wants to set the date for the auction. "So, I've got your number — thanks for coming over on such short notice. Thanks," Jessica said as she herded Kathy out the door.

"But... Oh, okay, well, bye, I guess. Lunch next week?"

Jessica shut the door before Kathy had finished her last word, the door almost hitting her as it closed behind her.

Kathy left, puzzled, shaking her head at her friend's odd behavior. *That girl needs to get out more,* Kathy thought as she drove off.

* * *

The phone rang.

"Jessica? Hey, this is Karl." His strained voice was lost on Jessica, who was anxious to convey what she had found.

"Karl, you know, I'm sorry, but you've just got to get back here right away. There's this room in the attic. Trunks... boxes... It's full of things that... that... I wish I'd never seen," Jessica stammered.

Damn. She knew.

"Yes, I just found out all about that from the papers that were in

Grandpa's safety deposit box. I was reading them on the plane. I don't know what this is all about, but I'm already heading back there. I'll be arriving in a couple of hours. I need you to lock yourself in the house and stay there until I get back. I know it's a lot to ask, but I need to talk to you about this, and I want you to show me what you've found."

Jessica wasn't expecting this. She was ready to pack up and get the hell out of Dodge. "Are you sure? I don't want to be here anymore. I want to go home."

"Oh. Of course. I'm sorry. Do you have to get home? I didn't even think of the inconvenience." Karl wanted her to stay.

Typical — no one does. Welcome to the world of real estate, Jessica thought.

"I don't want to take you away from your husband or your kids." Karl's voice trailed off.

Jessica didn't have a husband to go home to. Not anymore. No kids, no pets — what would she be going home to? What else did she have planned? As usual, nothing.

"Karl, I don't know what's going on here, and I really don't want to stay here, but I also don't really have any other plans, and, no, I don't have a family waiting for me. I'll be here," she whispered.

"What?" Karl said.

"I will be here," Jessica repeated. "Just get here as soon as you can."

"Okay, bye. I'll be there as soon as possible. And Jessica?" Karl said.

"Yes?"

"Thank you." Karl's sincerity came through loud and clear just before the line when dead.

* * *

The house was suddenly shrouded in an eerie silence. The only noise was the tick-tock of the grandfather clock in the hall, which seemed to get just a bit louder with each passing moment.

Jessica decided to take another tour of the house, this time looking through new eyes. The aura of the house was heavy, her footsteps echoing loudly through the hardwood hallways that connected the richly carpeted rooms.

The paintings and sculptures that had initially impressed her now taunted her. The genteel faces screaming at her — the ghosts of previous owners crying out to her. She came face to face with the forlorn painting over the fireplace in the living room. The portrait of the young woman locked gazes with her, the watery eyes seeming real. She could not pull herself away. The lips moved.

"Help me."

The whisper in her ear made her jump. She screamed and ran out of the room and into the kitchen. Shaken, she searched the cupboards until she found a glass and filled it with water, calming herself down.

Time to make a call. Jessica's hands shook as she dialed the number.

"Granny? Hi, it's Jessica. Yes, I'm okay. How's your hip? That's good to hear. Say, I was wondering..." A statue in the garden drew her gaze out the window over the sink. "What camp did you say that Grandpa was in during the war? Oh, I know, I know you don't like to think about that... I'll write it down this time and won't ever ask you again... Okay, great, thanks. One more thing... What town did he live in? I'm sorry, I didn't mean to make you cry. I'm sorry I upset you." Jessica wrapped up her call while writing furiously. "Thank you."

Jessica diverted the conversation. "Wasn't that a good dinner we had the other day? Oh, okay, well, if you're tired, I can let you go. Thanks, Granny. I love you."

* * *

Jessica's granny slowly hung up the phone, fumbling with the cradle. She gazed out the window, glassy eyed, still seeing the faces, the bodies, the screams that had haunted her since those days in her youth. A tear ran down her cheek.

*   *   *

Jessica folded the paper and put it in her pocket. She desperately wanted to run back up to the hidden attic room to check and see if she could find a match to her grandfather, but her body wouldn't cooperate. Instead, she steeled her will and resumed the tour of the house.

"Who owned you?" she asked the portrait over the fireplace. This time it didn't speak.

Silly girl, she berated herself. *Stop letting your imagination get away from you.*

She then addressed the portrait again. "I will get you back to where you belong. I promise." She left that room unaware that the painting's eyes still followed her.

*   *   *

Eventually, Jessica calmed her nerves. She had drifted off to sleep with the laptop resting on her legs in one of the overstuffed leather chairs in the living room. She startled awake as she heard the doorbell. In the short time she had rested, she had lived an eternity. The ghosts of her unsettling dreams dissipated as she shook off her drowsiness and returned to reality. Jessica made her way to the door, smoothing her hair and trying to straighten out the business suit.

"Who is it?" she asked and received the answer she had hoped for.

"Karl."

Jessica had never been so glad to see someone in her whole life.

Their eyes locked, realizing each had been completely changed in the few hours since they had first met.

"Show me."

She silently led him to the second-floor library. Jessica crossed the room to the bookcase, slid her fingers behind the edge, and gently pulled the case forward.

"Must be some sort of spring-loaded mechanism," Karl mused. "It just glides without a sound. I never knew it was here."

"Up here," Jessica said.

He followed her up the stairs into the secret room and gasped as she flipped the light switch to illuminate trunks and stacks of boxes. Karl turned toward Jessica and spoke.

"Listen, I'm sorry to have involved you in this. I had no idea..." His voice trailed off.

"Those other keys I gave you were in the safety deposit box, and I should never have given them to you."

Jessica eyed him suspiciously, motioning toward the boxes. "Do you know what's in them?"

"Well, no, not really, except my grandfather had some information about his past..." Karl didn't know how much to tell her. "What did you find?"

"Look for yourself." She handed Karl the keys.

Jessica didn't know what to expect from Karl. From her experience as a realtor, she was always cautious when in a home alone with a new client, positioning herself between them and the door as a plan of escape. She had trusted Karl, but she didn't know him, and this new information about his grandfather's past might make him do something. Gauging who to trust was a crucial skill in her profession, where she was often meeting strangers in vacant homes.

Her instincts had never let her down. More than once, she had called on her "showing buddy," a brawny male co-worker, to accompany her to a showing when she felt uncomfortable. Once a prospective "buyer" had driven off as soon as he saw she had a man with her. The danger was real, and she faced it every day.

Karl, however, was someone she felt comfortable with from the minute she had spoken to him on the phone. She trusted him, but as always, she followed her personal safety policy when meeting a new client. She had obtained all his contact information and a copy of his driver's license prior to meeting him and filed the appointment information at her office, just in case.

Either she had made a huge misjudgment about Karl, or they'd know who to find if she came up missing. Her mind was reeling, and she decided not to take any chances.

Karl fumbled with the key; the first footlocker unlocked with a click. It was obvious that what had been carefully stored for years had recently been rifled through. He picked up the uniform on the top of the pile, noting the swastika that glared at him. He quickly reviewed the papers, the identification, the birth certificates, and the photos. Karl rolled back on his haunches, taking it in.

Wow, it's true, Karl thought as he recognized an uncanny resemblance between himself and the young man in the photos.

No wonder I was so special to him, he thought. "I was the next him," Karl mumbled.

"Are you?" Jessica whispered anxiously, slowly backing away from him, closer and closer to the stairs.

"What?" Karl practically shouted. "No! Absolutely not. Jessica, please — I'm sorry you had to see all this, but you have nothing to be afraid of from me. I'm just finding all this out myself, and frankly, I'm feeling... a little... sick."

He tried to get to the stairs in time but didn't make it. As serious as the moment was, the sight of the gangly Karl trying to get up from his position and stumble through the attic looked goofy. Jessica was relieved to note that he was as sickened by it as she was, and as much as she tried to contain herself, she started to chuckle. Once she started, she couldn't stop, even though her sensibilities told her it was highly inappropriate. Karl, heaving and vomiting, cast a confused look her way.

"Okay, okay, I'm sorry," she said between chuckles, wiping a tear from her eye. "It's just that I did the same thing." Her hiccuppy laugh suddenly turned to sobs. "It's just too much..."

"Hey, no worries. I'd offer a hug, but I'm pretty sure you don't want puke all over you," Karl said, causing Jessica's sobs to alternate with laughter. "Let's decide what to do here. I'm going to see what other clothes I can find, and then we can figure out what's what."

* * *

"What does this mean?" They had regrouped and were back in the attic. Part of Jessica still wanted to flee, but the longer she stayed, the more she felt that she couldn't.

"Well, as far as I can tell, my 'wonderful' grandfather who taught me how 'special' I was, was a Nazi official entrusted with the protection of these boxes and trunks. Have you had a chance to look through any of them? I can't imagine what's so important about this stuff."

"I can," Jessica said. She had hours to try and make sense of it and did some online research before she fell asleep in the living room chair. "It's an inventory. A list of items obtained — or a better word, stolen — from Jews as they were taken from their homes. They were told to take whatever they could carry; anything left was confiscated. Then, even the items they carried with them were taken and documented at their destination, the concentration camps."

"No, that can't be." Karl, wrestling with disbelief, tore into the nearest box.

Ledger after ledger with titles stating the name of a city or a concentration camp, a bank, a salt mine — each neatly inscribed with names, addresses, dates, valuables. The businessman in him admired the precise record keeping.

"I think I'm going to be sick again." He sat back, breathing deeply, waiting for the nausea to pass.

"The question is. What do we do now?" Jessica said. "I mean, it's not really my business, but I can't just forget about all this…"

"Right…" Karl stood up, hands on his hips, surveying the attic's contents. "All right, I'm going to go out on a limb here and ask you to continue to help me with this. I don't want to tell anyone else about this, and, quite frankly, I don't think either of us really comprehends the implications here. From the information my grandfather left me, I know there are supposed to be people — associates of his — who are going to find me and 'help' me. I don't have any desire to meet with any of them. If they know I'm not willing to cooperate, well — we've seen what they can do…" He motioned toward the boxes.

Karl stopped and decided on a different approach.

"Well, then again, no. I appreciate all you've done, but this might get a little dangerous. I can't ask you to do anything more. You've been a tremendous help, but you can't get drawn into this any deeper than you already are. For your own safety."

"Whoa, aren't you overreacting just a little? I've had all afternoon to think about this and have an idea, if you're willing to listen. Plus, do you think there's any way I can just forget all of this and pretend it didn't exist? Don't think so."

"We'll see. What's your idea?"

"What we have here is more than an inventory of goods. It's documentation that specific items of value were taken from particular people. I'm guessing a lot of those property owners died in a gas chamber or in some other horrible way, but there may be descendants of those who survived who can have some minute form of restitution by having those items returned to them.

"Plus, I've done a little research online, and I'm sure these records are for real. So, this is the plan — first and foremost, we need to get these books somewhere safe and into the proper hands."

"Hm…" Karl mused, "if that is the case, we are playing with fire, and we won't be left alone here for very long. As far as we know, we could have guests at any minute."

Jessica had made a lot of sense, but he knew from his grandfather's paper that taking the information to the proper authorities would not make Grandfather's "Circle" very happy.

"I've got to say, Jessica, you've got a head on your shoulders," Karl said. "I have a feeling we don't have much time. Let's move the 'evidence' out of here."

Karl backed his rented SUV into the garage, and the two of them carted down every box and trunk from the attic to the garage and loaded them all into the back of the vehicle. Everything fit and was hidden from view under a blanket from the linen closet.

"The artwork," Jessica exclaimed after a few moments. "We can't just leave it. I'm convinced it's authentic and part of the confiscated goods. What should we do?"

"Well, where's your car?" Karl asked. "Give me your keys, and I'll pull it in the garage."

Since her occupation called for the ability to occasionally drive off-road, Jessica had the latest four-wheel-drive SUV, which could carry several prospective buyers over the roughest terrain. They folded down the seats, creating a larger bed than in Karl's rental. Jessica brought armloads of blankets, sheets, and pillows to the garage while Karl began bringing the artwork to wrap. Except for the largest statues, they were able to pack all of the collectibles into the back of Jessica's SUV, cushioning it with pillows around the sides.

With both vehicles packed and ready, Karl made one last trip up to the attic and secured the bookcase to the wall with a few nails while Jessica took a quick trip to the kitchen to pack as much food as they could eat on the road. Not much was still edible, except unopened crackers, Vienna sausages, some cheese, and a few bottles of wine.

"Does anyone know you were here?" Karl asked Jessica as he turned out the lights.

"Kathy was here to inventory the household for the estate sale. Aside from that, just my office. I always let them know as a precaution. I can call them in the morning and let them know I'll be on appointments."

"Well, that's about it, then," Karl said as they shut the last door and entered the garage. He stopped Jessica, taking both her hands in his. "I know I've said this before, but thank you. This is my problem, and I wish I didn't have to drag you into it. I will keep you safe."

Jessica looked at him, puzzled. "Thanks. I'm sure I'll be fine, but you're welcome."

"Just saying." Karl released her hands. "I think we need to find a safe place to leave the artwork and ride together in my car. Do you know of a garage or something we can use?"

"I have a garage," Jessica suggested.

"Well, that may not be the best idea. If they realize you're involved, that's the first place they'll go."

After a moment, Jessica lit up. "There's a twenty-four-hour, climate-controlled storage facility just off the interstate a couple miles from here that some of my clients have used when moving. It's very secure and expensive, but with the artwork, it'll be perfect. No fluctuations in temperatures, which is critical."

Karl looked at her sideways.

"I had an antique store. You can't just let artwork sit in a parked car somewhere. It would be ruined in a matter of hours."

"Sounds like that's where we need to go. Lead the way," Karl said before they left, one after the other, from the garage and quietly turned onto the dark, deserted boulevard.

* * *

Karl closed the overhead door of the storage unit they had just secured, locking Jessica's SUV safely inside. They pulled away from the facility just as the darkness of night was beginning to ebb, light teasing at the horizon as dawn threatened to break.

"Where do you live?" Karl asked.

Jessica shot him a curious glance.

Karl continued, "If you don't mind, can we stop there and decide exactly where we're heading while you grab anything you'll need to take with us?"

"No problem. It's not too far from here. I live just outside the metro area, and we're already headed in that direction."

After a short drive through continuous subdivisions, they arrived in a small town of century-old homes, completely surrounded by new subdivisions.

They passed the old town square, complete with gazebo, fountain, and statue, then parked in front of her sister's bed and breakfast across the street from Jessica's hundred ten-year-old Victorian home. Karl followed her up the wide steps to the wraparound porch and waited for Jessica to unlock her door. To his surprise, she opened it without a key.

"Not much happens around here. Most of the time, I just leave everything open. It's not as dangerous as you'd think. A small town has a million eyes looking out for you. It's the official pastime. It's like living under the eye of God. Everything you do is under scrutiny. If you look sideways, it's in the local paper. No lie. That's why I asked you to park across the street. A strange car at the B&B wouldn't raise an eyebrow, but if you parked in *my* driveway, well, let's just say tongues would wag."

Jessica was glad it was so early in the morning; no one would have seen them enter her house.

"Nice," Karl said, surveying her home. Original woodwork, vaulted tin ceilings and pocket doors reminiscent of Victorian days were offset by an eclectic mix of elegant modern furniture and antiques. Jessica had kept the best of her antique store after it closed; after her divorce, her heart wasn't in it.

He noticed several paintings on the walls, some with her name in the bottom right corner, others antique collectible prints from Remington, Elliott, Henke; centuries-old, hand-colored, lithograph illustrations and botanical prints.

"I can see you have a little background in collecting art."

"I've always liked beautiful things," Jessica said as Karl followed her through the parlors to the kitchen.

"Help yourself to the fridge. Make yourself something to eat. I'll be right back. Got to change and throw together a few things, just in case." Jessica turned around and handed Karl here briefcase. "Here's my laptop. Why don't you do a little research and see where we need to take these things. I don't think there's anywhere in Kansas City we can bring this stuff to, so maybe the next closest place?"

She grabbed an apple from the bowl on the counter and left him munching on some chips as he opened the laptop.

Karl scavenged the refrigerator, finding lunchmeat, cheese, and a bun, in which he threw together a sandwich and wolfed it down. He popped open a can of Coke to wash it down and turned his attention to the computer.

Now, where would I go if I were an important document needing to go somewhere safe? Karl thought.

He began using search words like "restoration of Jewish items" and "Nazi confiscated" to narrow it down to the most likely sources. He saved the pertinent information and concluded that the National Archives was where they needed to go. When Jessica returned to the kitchen, he was ready.

"Let's go," Karl said.

Jessica, not knowing exactly when she'd be back, locked her doors and left a quick note for her sister to check the mail and feed the cat just before they jumped into the car and began their quest.

4

AUSTRIA

The still, crisp morning air hung over the lake. A white-haired gentleman readjusted his soft brown velour jacket as he stood at attention on the veranda of the gleaming chateau, watching a swan appear through the last bit of the light fog dissipating over the glassy surface.

Hans Sprechter slowly pivoted and returned to his morning strudel and coffee; his thoughts transported back to what had transpired eons ago.

At the onset of the purification of Nazi-held countries, Hans had been handpicked to work in conjunction with other elite divisions, all directly under Himmler. Except for a handful of the very top of Hitler's chain of command, no one knew this council existed. No mention of it was ever documented, for the sole purpose of secrecy.

There were two divisions. Hans was one of three in command of one division, real estate. The other three in command controlled all other items of value. Their mandate was to hide and protect all assets until the New Reich emerged. Then, all the property and valuables would be liquidated to fund the new uprising when the New Holy Roman Empire was restored to its rightful place.

***

Hans had been disturbed by the news. To have all three of the Trusted Ones become... "ineffective" was unacceptable. No matter how much Henry Conrad wanted to choose his own successor, that individual had to be appointed by the Council. Unfortunately, the Council had become old, a fact that he was constantly reminded of with each pained step he took.

A new Council had been trained to take over, reminiscent of Hitler's Jungsturm — strong, able, young men who would stop at nothing to accomplish their task. Passing the baton to the new group was inevitable; the original members were dying off. As unsettling as turning over his life's work to someone else was, Hans found solace in the fact that the New Order would not die with him and his ancient comrades.

And now the grandson of Henry Conrad, AKA Reinhard Heydrich, would take the reins for that division, unless he could convince them otherwise. Hans had already given the orders to the others to make contact and evaluate his abilities before they'd accept him into the fold. Henry had insisted Karl was ready, but Hans trusted no one; not his wife, God rest her soul, not his worthless children, not his friends, nor his servants — only the old Council; there were too many secrets.

***

In 1940, when the Third Reich established Einsatzstab Reichsleiter Rosenberg (ERR), Hans was a young man. All the real estate the Empire acquired was kept secret to all except the Council; Himmler, Hitler, Goebbels, and Henry were directly over the Einsatzgruppen, who systematically rounded up Jews and other undesirables, herding them to the camps. As each was processed, the Einsatzgruppen kept a concise record of each name, address, and their possessions "acquired," which served two purposes; it kept a record of those put to death and also provided an inventory of goods.

Hitler's realm loved order and found the Einsatzgruppen to be most accurate in their accounting practices. Unfortunately, some records found their way into the wrong hands. They were used as evidence against some of their most important leaders at the Nuremberg Trials. But, officially, any other records were "destroyed."

Each city the Einsatzgruppen and the SS "purified" had its own ledger. Every item of value from each Jew's home, even the gold teeth pried loose from their mouths, was documented and stored. At first, storage facilities were the Reich's financial institution's vaults at the Reichsbank and other banks throughout Europe, but those soon overflowed, and they looked for other secure options as their treasure trove grew.

The amount of booty was incomprehensible. Only when the threat of an Allied invasion was upon them did the hordes of wealth get transported to their most secret hiding places. Ancient, fortified castles with secret rooms and impregnable dungeons were used as well as rooms carved out of solid rock in the underground salt or potassium mines that dotted Europe.

As a last resort of "if I can't have it, neither can you," much was unceremoniously dumped into the deep lakes dotting the region. It all quickly sank through the murky waters and came to rest on the silty bottom far below that would not be disturbed for years.

* * *

Hans still remembered when the inventory at the Merkers Mine in Austria became beyond their reach. *Ach, the losses that day.*

More than nine tons of gold, 8,200 gold bars made from melted-down Jewish possessions, fifty-five boxes of crated gold bullion, hundreds of bags of miscellaneous gold items, thirteen hundred bags of gold Reich currency, seven hundred eleven bags of US twenty-dollar gold pieces, British gold pounds and French gold francs, suitcases full of Jewish candlesticks, menorahs, gold fillings, jewelry, etc.

Soon afterward, the Allies discovered the Oberbayern treasure in

Bavaria with another nine tons of gold and bags of silver coins, seven hundred thirty gold bars, and crates laden with gold.

Meanwhile, the Nazis had frantically moved other caches and disposed of any witnesses.

They realized too late that loose tongues in Merkers and Oberbayern had cost them dearly. They would not let that happen again.

To remove such large quantities of valuables would surely be noticed. Even the hills had eyes, and only a select few could be trusted. Much of the original treasure was still hidden in secret with one sole purpose, and its time was near.

Hans' only desire was to live long enough to see the beloved New Nation restored to its former glory. At the current value, the gold and valuables would be worth billions.

Hans slowly forced his old body to rise from his chair. Knees, hips, you name it; whatever could be replaced, had been. But that left him with new joints surrounded by old tissue. Every step shot bolts of pain from his lower back to his heels.

Hans made his way through the French doors into his library. The leather-bound volumes were a treasure unto themselves. It was all his beloved Fuhrer's collection of work. All the authors that he loved and respected. Only these books had been worthy of the greatest libraries; all others should be burned and had been.

He waddled over to the old Victrola and picked out a thick, round, Richard Wagner celluloid, put it carefully in place, then cranked the side handle. He collapsed in an overstuffed chair, closing his eyes and drifting away to the strains of the music, relishing the memories of being in this very same room with those who had first appointed him to this position. Hitler himself, Himmler, Goebbels, and Reinhard Heydrich. His fingers gently moved as if conducting the strains that warbled from the Victrola.

He realized that he must speak directly with Henry Conrad's grandson, Karl. As much as he respected Henry and his ability to indoctrinate the boy, he knew that Henry's own son had rejected his teachings.

The son had been a danger. It had become clear that he was going to be a liability. For Henry's sake, the accident had to be quick and fatal. The car crash had hidden any traces of poison, and the ensuing fire eliminated any evidence that it was anything but an accident. Henry knew without being told that it had happened that way. He would have chosen to do the same and would have approved; in fact, they gave him the option. That child was a disgrace. His grandson, on the other hand, may prove useful.

* * *

Hans had attended the funeral for Karl's parents. That was the last time he had met with Henry in person. They had been at the funeral both to honor Henry and to observe Karl. And although Karl was evidently grieving for his poor excuse of parents, everything Henry had reported about the capabilities of the grandson had been proven by the months of observation prior to, and directly after, the parents' deaths.

Karl looked like the ideal Jungsturm candidate; Anglo Saxon to perfection, with his Germanic/Roman physique. The organizations he joined and his accomplishments were right in line with their secret society. He even exhibited the proper repulsion for anyone but his own kind. They would be watching him for potential leadership into the New Realm.

The ultimate agenda was to restore the now defunct Heiliges Römisches Reich (the Holy Roman Empire), reinstating thousands of years of heritage and power that had been dissolved in the early 1800s after the Napoleonic Wars.

The regime was renamed the German Confederation, which eventually became the German Empire. The Reichstag would once again restore proper order to what it should be, and would have been.

This is what the descendants of the last prince of the Reich had been anticipating for two hundred years. It was incomprehensible that their ancestor, Francis II, abdicated the throne, choosing to throw away a thousand years of selective royal breeding. Ever since the end of Charlemagne's line when Conrad I of Swabia was chosen for the honor of being the first Emperor of the Holy Roman Empire in 911, the Royal Line had been honored. And it would be again.

* * *

Karl and Jessica headed east. Their destination: the National Holocaust Museum in Washington, DC. Neither had slept well. Visions of concentration camps with children and families torn apart plagued Jessica's night while dreams of Nazi pursuers haunted Karl's. They drove in subdued silence.

Jessica wasn't sure why she was driving through Missouri with a man she didn't know just two days ago.

Wow, has it just been a day? she thought. It had seemed so much longer. So much had transpired in the twenty-four hours since she had taken his call.

Their plan, Karl had decided, was to drive nonstop, as far as possible, until they could drive no more. Then they'd get a room somewhere off an exit; with two bedrooms so he would be close enough to protect her if necessary. Jessica thought he was overreacting a bit, but his chivalry didn't go unnoticed. In fact, she kind of liked it.

Karl had been wondering why Jessica had seemed so necessary to have along. She knew too much to be left behind. Not that Karl distrusted her, but she could be in danger just by the brief association with him, and that angered him.

What was his grandfather thinking? What "larger destiny" did he have in mind? It was unsettling. If Grandpa was a Nazi, the implications were too vast to comprehend.

Karl's thoughts kept being interrupted by business calls from his office. He eventually had his secretary field his calls once he realized that he was far too distracted to focus on anything else.

In the business world, Karl was analytical, known for his ability to assess a situation, analyze the problem, and arrive at a concise solution with such accuracy and clarity that he had a reputation as "the Fixer."

From the information his grandfather had revealed, coupled with the documents and childhood "training," Karl knew his grandfather's plan was an ominous one. One he wasn't willing to participate in it, whatever it was.

Karl had a great desire to distance himself as much as possible from any connection to his grandfather's associates. Professionally, it would be disastrous, and personally, he couldn't stomach it. Not only didn't he want to be associated with these people, he also wanted to right any wrongs they and his grandfather might have done.

Delivering the ledgers to the authorities would absolve him of any responsibility, and the good folks at the Holocaust Museum would be those he trusted most right now to do that.

* * *

Jessica watched the beauty of the land pass by as they sped eastward. They had been traveling in a comfortable silence, interrupted occasionally by her real estate calls.

As a realtor, Jessica had learned to assess people almost immediately. Because of the misguided public distrust of realtors, many of her clients were close-mouthed and initially did not reveal everything to her about their plans or financial situation. This frustrated Jessica to no end, leaving no other option than to rely on her own powers of observation and instincts to piece together an accurate picture of what her clients' motivations really were.

Although she tended to believe the best in people, the adage "buyer's lie" had been proven out to her more than once. Jessica's assessment of her clientele culminated in their body language, the subtle tics of the face, and the shifty eyes.

Once she knew their insecurities, she would get to the task of overcoming those obstacles. Eventually, her clients realized that they could relax and trust her, knowing she was operating in their best interest.

* * *

"How 'bout some lunch?" Karl asked as took an exit ramp off the interstate. "I'm going to fill up the tank, and if it's all the same to you, let's stretch our legs now and then go through a drive-thru so we don't lose any time."

"Sure, works for me," Jessica said.

Karl stopped at an ATM before they left Kansas City, pulling out the maximum amount from his bank account. He did the same from the gas station's ATM machine. His accounts seemed bottomless. His job had a generous salary, but he was also frugal.

They were soon back on the interstate. Karl was munching the last French fry when a thought struck him. "I wonder how extensive Grandpa's network is. I mean, the guy at the bank, Heinrich — well, Heinrich knew me, expected me. That bank has branches throughout the United States. I even use the branch near me in Chicago..." Karl's voice trailed off for a moment. "In fact, I believe Grandpa set that account up for me."

He shook his head. "I'm getting paranoid, and I don't like it." Karl set the cruise control up a notch.

"What are you saying?" asked Jessica, shifting to face Karl as he drove.

"What if these people who 'will be in contact with me' somehow discover we've taken off with the art and books? Can they track us?"

Jessica gave it some thought. "Well,... I guess anytime you use your credit card or access your bank account, it could be traced. I know that in real estate we're taught to always have our cell phones, just in case, God forbid, someone needs to trace our location if we go missing. The signal to the cell tower can be used to track you down."

"Uh... not good," Karl said. "So, hypothetically, if they could know that we were in Kansas City and now are in Illinois, there's no way they'd know we were on our way to DC. They'd think I was going home to Chicago. So, let's assume the worst, that someone is trying to track us. I'm not going to use my gas card anymore. I have plenty of cash. I don't want you to use the ATM either. I'll tell my secretary to tell everyone I don't have cell phone coverage where I am, so we can't be tracked that way and will be under the radar. I have Skype, so if I need to make a call, we can do it via computer."

"Okay, now I'm freaking out," Jessica wheezed. "I wasn't too paranoid before, but I do agree, it's a possibility. I'm *sure* your grandpa's people wouldn't want this stuff in the hands we intend to put it in. But as of right now, they don't know you don't plan to cooperate, so if they call you... maybe its best that you put all calls into voicemail. You can play along with them until the information is safely in the proper hands."

Karl thought about this scenario for a moment, the wheels moving faster and faster. "Agreed. If they find us and realize I'm not going to play their game, well, that just wouldn't be good."

They drove again in silence, the steady hum of the tires on the road the only sound.

"Then again, we may be overreacting just a bit. But if we operate as if the worst-case scenario is playing out, then at least we're better prepared to deal with it if it is indeed the case." Jessica sighed heavily.

* * *

"They are in Illinois," the suit reported to his mentor behind the huge mahogany desk. "He just used an ATM again."

"So, he's headed home in a car rather than by plane..." The boss' voice trailed off. "But you said he flew home to Chicago yesterday afternoon and then caught the next flight back to Kansas City? Strange."

Something about this whole scenario unsettled him. He was accustomed to being suspicious of everyone's movements. He had learned to trust no one, and anything out of the ordinary was a big red flag.

"I think it's time we gave Mr. Karl Conrad a call."

The suit left, and the man behind the desk sat back in his chair a moment, steepling his hands under his chin. He had always disagreed with Henry Conrad about the path his grandson was to take, but the old man was adamant.

He just wanted his bloodline to dominate, he thought. *The old fool was blinded to all the other options.*

In his mind, they had the most obvious leader right in front of them.

I am the best-suited and should — no, will — be in control. And now that the old man is gone, I only need to take care of the other old guy, and all the stumbling blocks are gone. Yes, he thought with a smile, *it's all coming together as I had hoped.*

* * *

The visitors to Henry Conrad's home noted the missing artwork. So far, the secret room had not been found, but an extensive search of the premises was underway.

"Where are the records?" he shouted into the phone. "Take every book off the shelf in that library and examine them. They *must* be found."

Karl's condo was ransacked in Chicago. The security system for the building was not a deterrent, nor was the security guard.

The search team was a stealthy bunch. They would be waiting for Karl to arrive home, however long that took. His office held nothing of interest, but listening devices were placed in various hidden spots, as well as a tiny camera hidden on a shelf between a portrait of Karl with a sailboat and another with a huge sailfish caught off the coast of St. John's.

Karl's secretary had believed the fabricated story of them being old school buddies that were anxious to meet with Karl but wanted it to be a surprise. She agreed to let them know as soon as she heard from him and to honor their desire for secrecy.

But Karl had already stopped calling in.

* * *

They were travelling on Interstate 64, almost to Louisville, Kentucky. At every gas stop since they'd realized their vulnerability, they paid strictly using cash. Jessica's phone rang incessantly. After initially trying to field the usual barrage of real estate questions, she realized that her mind kept wandering, her concentration shot.

Jessica set her phone on silent and tucked it into her purse.

They'll just have to wait, she thought as ideas danced through her mind.

"I'd say just about the time we get to Louisville, they'll be expecting me to arrive at my home in Chicago. That is, if they're watching for me. Any time after that, we will have to get serious about reaching our destination as soon as we can," Karl said as he opened a Slim Jim and waved it at her. "Want one?"

"Um, no thanks," Jessica replied, wrinkling her nose. "Interesting smell. I was beginning to wonder if lunch wasn't sitting well in your stomach or something. I'll stick to my mustard pretzels," she said, licking the mustard dust off her yellow fingertips. "I think it's wise to err on the side of caution and just assume we are in a race to get there, and they don't want us to. Have you thought about the rental car issue?"

"Rental car issue? If you mean if they'd be able to trace it, then yes, sure I've thought about it..." Karl was now realizing they could easily be traced. "The good thing is that they don't know about you yet, Jessica. We can turn this car in and rent something else in your name. No, they'll figure that one out pretty quickly by asking the rental guy... I'm not sure how we can do this." Karl mulled this over for a few moments.

After a contemplative lull in the conversation, Jessica's face lit up.

"I know. Let's rent a car in my name from a different car rental company. Unload all these boxes from your rental into mine, and by the time they figure it all out, we'll be in DC, safe and sound," Jessica offered. "That way they only track us as far as Louisville. Maybe you can even buy a plane ticket for the next day to Chicago and reserve a hotel room. You can check in, and then we'll leave. *That* would throw them off track."

"Wow, I like the way you think," Karl replied.

I've read every Robert Ludlum, Tom Clancy, and John Grisham

book that's come out," Jessica quipped. "It's easier to think of this situation in those terms, like it's not really happening to me, with the WWJBD mindset."

"Huh?"

"You know, what would Jason Bourne do?"

"Ha! I've gotta say this about you. You definitely think differently. But in a good way."

For the first time in a day and a half, Karl chuckled. "Okay, sounds like we've got a plan. Let's find a car rental place before they close for the day."

Karl took Interstate 65 south to the airport, found a hotel, checked in, booked a flight from Jessica's phone, stopped by Budget to rent a car for Jessica, returned his to Hertz after transferring their load, and got on their way again in record time. Karl made one last call to his secretary, informing her that he was meeting with a client in Louisville and would fly home to Chicago the next night.

"Whew, now I can relax," Karl said after he came back and they were safely driving away. "We're covered for another day. Let's drive as long as we can, then find a place to sleep for a few hours."

"Works for me."

Jessica was still wondering why she felt compelled to leave with him without question. The need to do the right thing for once may have overpowered her general sense of safe procedure. She trusted him and was glad Karl needed to get their cargo into the correct hands; it was a mandate she felt in her bones. Knowing this, she realized she never would have begun this arduous journey with the stranger from Chicago, no matter how attractive he was.

The adrenaline kept them moving forward, alert and awake. Karl would not let himself get complacent by thinking that they were safe. He would not let his guard down; not only to protect the historical records they were hauling, but also to protect Jessica, who had been drawn into this mess because of him.

It's always the stupid little things that screw things up, he thought, *like those criminals that break into a place but accidentally drop their driver's license...*

Karl's thoughts wandered to what would happen once the records were transferred. The artwork they left in the climate-controlled storage unit could be released to the proper authorities — then what? Grandpa's cohorts would definitely not be happy about what was about to transpire.

Karl's only regret was unnecessarily dragging Jessica into this mess.

* * *

"What was your grandfather's real name?" Jessica asked. "I might as well make myself useful and pull information off the internet about him while we're driving."

"Reinhard Heydrich," Karl said and then spelled it out for her.

Yikes, she thought after the search results popped onto her screen. There were a ton of hits. She clicked the first option.

"Let's see..." Jessica began, "Reinhard Heydrich. One of Hitler's elite SS men in charge of the Einsatzgruppen, established in 1939. Wikipedia says that Einsatzgruppen was a task-force intervention group formed by Himmler and operated by the SchutzStaffel, SS, before and during WWII, in full force in 1941. Their principal task was the annihilation of Jews, Gypsies, Soviets, and political commissars. There were four main death squads that spread through the German occupied territories. From their own records, the Einsatzgruppen killed more than a million Jews, execution style. According to firsthand accounts, those they gathered up were told they were going to be relocated so they should bring some food and whatever valuables they could carry to a certain location. Once there, the food and valuables were taken from them, and they were herded into transport vehicles."

Nausea overcame Jessica, but she could not stop reading.

"Once the Jews were eliminated in one area, the Nazis moved to the next community, repeating the process. To make it easier on the soldiers who had wives and children at home and were traumatized over killing innocent Jewish women and children, the Einsatzgruppen began transporting their victims in a specially designed truck that would gas the occupants en route.

"They found that this method was not much of an improvement, as the victims would beat on the sides of the truck, crying out until they succumbed to the fumes. Plus, at their destination, the soldiers, or other Jews forced to assist, had to unload the bodies, some of which would fall out as the doors opened, further traumatizing the German soldiers.

"A progression to concentration camps then occurred as more 'new and improved' methods of killing their victims were developed.

"Oh, man, this is nasty..." Jessica interjected, then continued. "There were reports of earth explosions from the mass grave sites shortly thereafter as the bodies decayed and produced methane gas, causing the ground to heave where the trenches had been dug. To destroy any evidence of the killings, teams were sent out to exhume the bodies and experimented with several options as to how to best dispose of the remains completely, to cover their tracks.

"A funeral pyre was built using layer after layer of decomposed bodies on shelves of logs soaked with flammable liquid and set ablaze. The remaining bones were put through a bone-crushing machine. These trial-and-error methods of killing and disposing of millions of bodies helped create a more efficient manner of processing bodies through the concentration camps."

Jessica read without emotion. The sordid information had made her numb, a hard knot had formed in the pit of her stomach, and she realized that she couldn't continue. Her head pounded, and she felt ill.

"I can't do this. Can we pull over for a minute? Like, *now!*"

Karl swung over to the shoulder of the interstate and screeched to a halt. Jessica flung open the door and jumped out. She walked into a field, taking in deep breaths of fresh air, fighting the nausea.

Jessica had the car to her back with the field in front of her, edged by a thick forest. She saw something move in the trees. A deer? She saw another movement and focused on the image. There was another, then another — she couldn't look away, completely transfixed as the scene came into focus. She saw people, stumbling quickly through the woods, twenty or so; fathers, mothers, children, frail old men, and women. The last in line glanced quickly behind him. Jessica followed his line of sight to a group of men in uniform with a few others in civilian clothes, all with guns. Behind them stood a group of young children.

Jessica's gaze drifted back to the head of the line; they had come to a stop and were at the edge of a huge trench. The children were wailing, their mothers holding them tightly. Prayers were sent up in singsong Hebrew. Some were emotionless, some were hysterical. Shots rang out and the people slumped and fell into the abyss, landing with a thud on layers of others, some of which were still alive, all of which were covered in blood.

The soldiers then forced the non-Jewish village children to run on top of the pile of bodies to stomp them down, compressing the pile, making room for others. A scream drew Jessica's eye. The hand of a wounded, trapped victim reached up and tried to grasp a child's ankle. Jessica followed the bloody hand down the arm to the face of the woman, alive but trapped under the pile of dead bodies. Jessica's eyes locked with the hapless victim.

"Help me," she mouthed just as dirt showered her head, blurring Jessica's view.

Then everything went dark.

* * *

"Jessica…" She heard Karl's voice far, far away, as if at the end of a long hall. "Jessica, wake up!"

She slowly opened her eyes, disoriented. Jessica lay on the ground in the field by the car. As she regained her composure, she quickly sat up and quickly glanced toward the woods.

Only trees.

She heaved a sigh of relief.

"What's wrong? You look terrified," Karl said with concern as he helped Jessica to her feet. "What just happened?"

Jessica, not knowing how to convey what happened to her into words, just shook her head. "I'm not sure..." She slowly got back into the car. "Let's just go."

"All right, I think I've heard enough for now, and I don't want you getting sick again, so how about if I do some more research myself when we find a place to stay?" Karl suggested as they got underway.

Jessica thought this was a great idea.

5

MARRIOTT HOTEL
MIDWAY THROUGH THE UNITED STATES

Karl deposited Jessica's bag and briefcase into one of the suite's bedrooms, then dropped his bag on the floor of the other. Jessica had already begun making a pot of coffee but stopped midstream. "Now, I really need you to tell me what happened back there."

"I don't know if I can," she said.

"Okay," Karl said, taking her hands and pulling her to the sofa. "Let's just sit down, and I want you to try."

Jessica took a deep breath and recounted her experience. "It was the same feeling that overcame me in your grandfather's home, but worse. It's as if I was right there witnessing it." Tears streamed down her cheeks. "It was beyond horrible. The guards acted as if it was just another day. Mission accomplished — time to clock out and have a cigarette — all in a day's work. And those poor children. Those who died, and for the poor little kids that were forced to stomp those bodies down... Traumatized for life. How does a memory like that go away?"

What she'd seen poured out of her.

"Wow, at first I couldn't get you to talk, and now I can't get you to stop." Karl tried to lighten the atmosphere but failed miserably.

Jessica shot him daggers from her eyes.

"Sorry. Hey, it's okay. It sounds like you have a healthy dose of empathy, and that's not necessarily a bad thing. Where did you hear that story? Was that part of what you found on the internet?"

"No, I never knew anything like that had ever happened before. It was as if I was actually there, like watching it happen in a movie, like a dream. I didn't look up anything else but what I read to you."

They sat there in silence, thinking.

"Well, let's get those tears dried up," he said as he brushed her cheeks. "I need a shower. Do you? Well, honestly, I think you do."

Jessica scowled at him.

"Hey, just kidding."

"You know, a cup of coffee and a hot shower do sound pretty good right now," Jessica said, getting up off the couch. "You're welcome to use my laptop if you want to look up some more information on Gramps," she said as she shut the bathroom door.

* * *

Karl entered Jessica's bedroom and took the briefcase from her bed into the living area.

Laptop removed, he searched the briefcase pockets for the power cord and battery. Reaching into one section, his hand touched something. A bewildered expression crossed his features. Two of his grandfather's ledgers were tucked into the pocket.

"What the...?" Karl muttered under his breath. "Why in the world would she take these?"

He stormed into the bathroom. The room was a haze of strawberry shampoo-scented steam.

Jessica let out a small yelp and grabbed for a towel as the bathroom door slammed open. "What do you think you're doing?" she screeched.

"Explain this." Karl, clearly agitated, waved the books at her. "Why did you steal these? I thought I could trust you."

Karl's anger overruled his usual decorum He realized too late that he had placed her in a compromising position. He looked away but held his ground.

Jessica wrapped herself in the towel and stepped out of the shower. Seeing the ledgers, she opened her mouth and then shut it again.

"I... I can explain," she began.

"Go ahead." Karl's nostrils flared.

Jessica was loosely clad in the towel, her skin rosy from the heat of the shower, the water beading on her smooth shoulders.

"Karl, I'm Jewish."

* * *

"My grandfather's family all died in a concentration camp — all except him. My grandmother, well, she had a similar story." Tears streamed down her already wet face. "I took two books out of the boxes before you got home. One is from the camp he was in, and one from the town they lived in before being taken to Terezin. I just wanted to know to see if I could find their names, and then I was going to give them back. I'm sorry. I planned on putting them back before you ever found out..." Her voice was not much more than a whisper.

Karl felt helpless to eliminate her sorrow. He wrapped her in his arms in a vain attempt to heal her wounds. "I'm sorry... You should have said something."

She buried her head against his shoulder, relieved, and let herself release every bit of the pent-up anxiety that had built up over the past few days. She fit perfectly in his arms, and he held her tightly, one arm encircling her and the other stroking her damp hair.

"I'm sorry," Karl whispered, and her soft sobbing was the only sound for a few minutes.

He let her cry until she had no more inside her. Jessica's body fell limp against his chest as she succumbed to the physical and emotional exhaustion. They swayed back and forth, Karl still whispering, "It's okay," until her warm, curvaceous body pressed up against his started to affect him. He gently pushed her away from him, brushed a stray hair from her face, and looked her in the eyes.

"Listen, we're both exhausted. Let's get you to bed. I mean, I'll help you get to your bed in your bedroom. I'll be going to my bed... in my bedroom..." he stammered.

Jessica put a finger to his lips. "Thank you."

She was drained, emotionally and physically, the adrenaline that had kept her going nonstop for the past thirty-six hours finally subsiding. Her eyes slammed shut as soon as Karl tucked her into her bed, still clad in just her towel.

"Night," he said, brushing her cheek softly with his fingers. "Sleep well. Only good dreams for you."

Karl turned the light off and quietly shut her door. He should have also gone to bed but knew he'd just toss and turn.

Might as well continue what I had started to do, Karl thought as he sat down at the desk with Jessica's laptop.

He started by googling Reinhard Heydrich. The image of the young man in uniform was undoubtedly his grandfather. The reality of the charade hit home. Karl spent the next hour educating himself about the man he didn't know. By the time Karl's head jerked awake for the third time, he decided to succumb. He was asleep within moments.

* * *

The tattoo on the burly man who trudged in the mud in front of her moved slightly to the right and left as his bicep flexed. The rose with the winding vine was lovely, but the odd combination of his rough stature with the flower for a tattoo seemed out of place. She fixated on seeing the rose move each time he lifted the heavy sledgehammer and slammed it down onto the rocks in the quarry, crushing them.

Then he was gone, and she was walking in a grey world. The buildings were grey, the sky was grey, the people all wore grey with black striped outfits; their grey sullen pallor, dark circles under their eyes. She meandered toward the woods on the other side of the fence topped with rolled barbed wire. A grey house stood just beyond the fence. She stood there looking at the house, her eyes drawn to a single red rose in the grey garden just beyond her confinement.

A voice startled her. There was a man standing in front of the house.

"Oh, you're a pretty one..." The heavy German accent made her shiver. "I want to show you my collection, my dear, come with me..."

Although every fiber of her being wanted to run, she could not. The barbed-wire fence parted, and she floated toward him as if drawn by a magnet. She followed him to the house, the red rose wilting as she passed, up the porch stairs, through the parlor, and into a room set up as some sort of display area indicative of a museum.

"I think you'll like my collection..."

His sinister voice made her skin crawl as she unwittingly viewed the various items.

"Do you like my pretty lamp?" he asked, stopping near a table that held books bound in leather, leather cigarette lighters, leather pen holders.

Kind of ordinary items to be in a museum, she thought, but then her eyes rested on the lampshade. It was leather also, and when she focused on the design on the shade, she realized where she had seen the rose and vine before. "No!" she screamed.

* * *

Jessica sat upright in her bed, the last throes of the scream in her throat, unsure if her voice was only in her dream or if she had screamed. Panting, her heart pounding wildly in her chest. It had only been a dream. Her stomach knotted again, the same as in the house and before when she'd had the vision in the woods. She glanced around at the darkness surrounding her, still seeing wispy creatures swirling around the room, gradually diminishing. She knew if she closed her eyes again, worse images would reappear, so she got out of bed and went to the kitchenette.

Karl had fallen asleep on the couch with the laptop propped on his chest. Jessica gingerly removed the computer, intending to shut it off. Her thumb brushed against the keyboard, bringing the dormant computer back to life.

Karl had drifted off while reading about his grandfather. He had researched as far into his history as when he was commander of the concentration camp, Theresienstadt.

Jessica's eyes were drawn to that name. "I can't believe it," she whispered.

A loud snore made her jump. Karl rolled over on the couch, his rhythmic breathing indicating he was still fast asleep.

Theresienstadt, also known as Terezin, was where her granny had said that her grandfather had been interred. Jessica read:

June 10, 1940, Gestapo takes control of Theresienstadt and installs a prison in the small fortress. By November 24, 1941, the site was transformed into the Walled Ghetto, having the aim of providing a frontage, hiding the extermination of Jews. Under the command of the SS leader, Reinhard Heydrich. Jessica sucked in her breath. *For the outside world, Terezin was presented by the Nazis as a model Jewish colony, but inside, it was a concentration camp, used as a transit site for Jews on their way to Auschwitz for extermination.*

Jessica slammed the laptop shut. The sudden noise made Karl grunt.

* * *

"Hello?" The tall gentleman answering the door at Henry Conrad's home had finally responded to Kathy's persistent ringing. She had seen a black Mercedes outside and knew that eventually someone would come to the door.

"Hi, I'm Kathy. You must be Karl. Jessica asked me to drop these off to you when I was finished pricing everything. Just let me know when you'll be ready to do the sale." Kathy handed the folder to the man she had mistaken for Karl. "Have you talked to Jessica today? I haven't been able to reach her. If you talk to her, would you have her call me?"

"Of course," he replied. "By the way, do you have Jessica's number? I can't find it."

"Sure thing." Kathy fished around in her purse for one of Jessica's business cards. "Say, I've got to tell you that I'm very impressed with the quality of the artwork. If it wasn't for a few knicks and dents, I'd think they were the real thing." She handed him Jessica's card.

"Um, thanks, uh, Kathy," he said, glancing at the folder with a gold sticker emblazoned with *Kathy Malz, Estate Sales*. "Thanks for all you've done. Believe me, you really helped me figure things out," he said, clearly wanting her to leave. "We'll be in touch. I'll give Jessica your regards."

"But... I still have some questions..." Kathy's voice trailed off as the door slammed shut mid-sentence. "Eccentric," Kathy muttered as she walked down the sidewalk, got in her car, and drove away.

His phone rang.

"He wasn't on the plane. He didn't board, but his rental car was returned to the airport. We've lost him," the agitated man on the other end of the phone told him.

"I believe we may have another lead. I'll contact you again soon," he said and disconnected.

Jessica Sinclair, Realtor, Multi-Million-Dollar Producer, the business card read.

"Hm... I think it's time we had a little... *consultation*," he mused as he dialed her number.

"Hello, this is Jessica," he heard and began to say something but was interrupted by, "I'm sorry I've missed you, but your call is very important to me. Please leave your name, number, and nature of your call, and I will return your call as soon as possible... *Beep*."

His short temper, already pushed to its limits, got the best of him. He had to quickly regain composure to leave a credible message on Jessica's phone.

"Yes... Jessica. I have a serious interest in a house you just listed. Oh, you may be interested to hear that your friend, Kathy Malz, just dropped off the estate sale information... wanting to hear from you soon... or I could just pay Kathy a visit to *gather* information... I think you'll prefer to call me *before* I need to do that. My name is Stefan, and I will be anxiously awaiting your call..."

* * *

Jessica's cell phone had been in a dead zone for the past hour. Once it regained reception, it beeped to indicate she had a message. Although not mentally prepared to answer questions from clients, she was still checking her messages for anything urgent. She had missed eleven calls, mostly inquiries about her listings and contracts. More than a few were from Kathy.

"Hey, Jessica, where are you? I have your quote ready..." Jessica listened to the first sentence of each message then passed to the next. The blood drained out of her face as she listened to the next message from Kathy.

"Hey, Jessica. I just met Karl at the house and gave him the estimate on the property..." The rest of the message trailed off as if she were in a dream. The next one, left by Stefan, made her blood run cold. The phone fell out of her hand.

"Shit!" she hissed as she finally exhaled. "Shit, shit, shit!"

"What's wrong?" Karl asked nervously. "What did your message say?"

"They know about me," Jessica whispered incredulously. Until a minute ago, she thought she was under the radar, but now a prickly, paranoid panic crept up her spine, tightening her chest and constricting her throat.

"They know I'm involved," she said with a sickening realization that suddenly nothing in her life as she knew it mattered anymore.

* * *

"Can you tell where they are?" Stefan furiously demanded of the technician pecking away at the computer's keyboard.

Adam, the IT tech, was working as fast as he could, continually wiping his sweaty palms on his pants. Stefan Krumholz's need for information made him nervous. Beads of sweat were on Mr. Krumholz's brow, which were quickly duplicated on Adam's forehead.

"Almost... there..." Adam told Stefan, hoping that would keep him at bay. A chirp sounded from the computer, and a red blinking arrow appeared. A wave of relief washed over his whole body, and he relaxed a little, regaining a bit of confidence. "Looks like she is in Harrisonburg, Virginia."

"What?" Stefan growled. "What is she up to? Keep at it. Let me know where she goes."

Stefan Krumholz turned on his heel, muttering, "He's not going to like this..."

* * *

Karl did not notice the black sedan as it fell into traffic several vehicles behind them.

"Greg Simpson, please." Jessica had just spent half an hour on her phone, locating the document expert at the National Archives. "Mr. Simpson, this is Jessica Sinclair... I have an unusual request..."

* * *

Greg hung up the phone in his office in Washington, DC, glad he had not left early that day as he had planned. If what she had said was true, they had their missing link.

After Patton's division had liberated Germany in WWII, much of the gold and valuables stolen from the Jews and other victims had been recovered; billions of dollars' worth in today's prices. But what was lacking was accurate documentation for exactly where and whom the goods had been stolen from. The artwork and antiques removed from museums and public places was easy enough to track down and return, but most of the millions of pieces of gold, silver, art, jewelry, and artwork came from private homes. Even if any descendants had survived the executions and camps, there just wasn't any definitive way to prove what belonged to whom. Lawsuits were still being filed from Jewish survivors and their families. Most ended up being dismissed due to lack of evidence. All proof of ownership had been destroyed.

Currently stored in secure vaults and museums, these items remained, patiently waiting to be returned to their rightful owners.

Greg could barely contain his excitement but forced himself to rein in his emotions. He couldn't allow himself to think that they were bringing him the only existing records to connect those dots. Greg, thinking it wise to not be the only one with such important knowledge, placed one phone call.

"I had to tell someone. Can you get over to my office *right now*?"

* * *

Karl had now picked up on the dark sedan tailing them. During the past half hour, he had consistently seen it lagging behind them as he fluctuated his speed, confirming his suspicions.

"Listen, Jessica, hypothetically, how could someone know exactly where we are right now?" Karl tentatively asked.

"What?" Jessica pivoted her head around to look behind them.

"No, don't look." Karl's sharp tone made Jessica obey.

"Hypothetically?" Fighting the urge to hyperventilate, Jessica regained her composure and took a deep, calming breath. "All right, let's assume we have company. We're over an hour away from our destination, and getting there *must* happen. The only way I can think of that they could track us is by the GPS in our cell phones. Don't ask me how I know. I watch too many private-investigator shows. They'd have to have some good connections to be able to do it, though."

"Well, if that's the case, let's make a call to someone who can help us and then figure out how we're going to lose our tail." Karl's mind was working at lightning speed.

They made another call to Greg Simpson, telling him everything; how they came to be in possession of the ledgers and who Karl's grandfather really was, even the neo-Nazi plan to restore the Holy

Roman Empire. They told him the make and model of their rental car, their exact location, and then waited for the next step.

* * *

"Simon, sit down. The story I'm about to tell you is positively unbelievable," Greg Simpson blurted as his long-time friend and mentor, Simon Thaldorf, arrived.

Greg began his account by telling of an event that was of historical record.

"In February, 1942, Reinhard Heydrich was assassinated by the Czech resistance soldiers, who had parachuted into Nazi territory as he was driving down a road. According to what we know from the records, Heydrich did not die directly from the gunshot wounds. In fact, he wasn't mortally wounded at all and had enough strength to return fire at his assailants. A week later, it was reported that Heydrich died from blood poisoning caused by debris embedded in his tissue from his car at the time of the shooting. A huge funeral was held, since Heydrich was one of Hitler's elites. Hitler had publicly criticized Heydrich for exposing himself to danger by riding in an open car, taunting death."

"So, Heydrich evidently *didn't* die from blood poisoning but was kept in hiding, still running some of the Third Reich's most gruesome ethnic cleansing, but safe from assassins since he was already, quote, *dead*. After the United States and Allies liberation of Nazi held territories occurred and many were put to trial in Nuremburg, Reinhard Heydrich followed the *Ratline* to the United States. They had a kind of underground railway for Nazi war criminals. That was the Ratline, and that's how so many were secreted out of Germany into other countries. The Nazis who escaped this way were referred to as Ratliners."

Simon Thaldorf listened with fascination. His life work consisted of tracking down the aging Nazis in hiding all over the world. He was familiar with the Ratlines and had been successful in tracing those in hiding. It was tedious work that took decades, but he was patient;

those he tracked had to be held accountable. Simon was torn between the forgiveness his faith required him to bestow and the desire to give these monsters what they deserved — the same treatment they had heartlessly inflicted on tens of thousands. In the end, the realization that he would have sunken to their level, had always guided his actions. After locating a war criminal, he resisted the urge for revenge and merely turned the pathetic prisoner over to the proper authorities to be tried for their past crimes. He had lists of the ones that escaped at the end of the war, and one by one he had diligently followed the clues to uncover these criminals in hiding.

Heydrich's name was not found on any list. That made Greg and Simon wonder if there were other such "ghosts" still out there.

"They're being followed," Greg told Simon. "I'm sure Karl and Jessica don't realize the great importance of what they carry and what lengths those chasing them will go to prevent them from reaching us. Do you know of anyone who can intercept their pursuers?"

"Intercept? Like, as in, get rid of them? Yes, as a matter of fact, I do." Simon made a call.

Soon, another nondescript vehicle fell into traffic several hundred feet behind the dark sedan, trailing Karl and Jessica.

* * *

Karl had been plotting a diversion, once he received Greg's call that their plan was in action.

"Turn off our phones, please, my dear, and tighten your seatbelt," Karl said, grasping the opportunity. They were coming up on Washington, DC, and the crazy eight-lane traffic that surrounded the capitol. As soon as two semis lined up in tandem, Karl passed them on the left, quickly changing lanes and darting far to the right, crossing three lanes of traffic as soon the trucks blocked their pursuer's line of sight.

Once Karl was around the semis, he slowed down dramatically in the far-right lane and took the exit for the Beltway. The slip was smooth and executed perfectly, although the daring maneuver made

Jessica queasy. The dark sedan continued along the other interstate, but the driver of the second vehicle, which Simon had sent, was expecting something like this and was far enough behind both to see the quick exit and follow Karl and Jessica onto the Beltway. This vehicle raced up ahead of Karl's vehicle to guide them safely along the interstate to the National Archives.

* * *

"You idiot," Hans Sprechter barked into the phone. "Get them back!"

This was turning into a bumbling disaster. He panted as he waved his cane, threatening the aide who tried to come to his assistance.

"Find them," he hissed as he lowered himself into the wingback chair, reaching for the oxygen that he suddenly needed. Inhaling deeply, the stars that were beginning to dance before his eyes slowly faded. He had to try alternative means to locate the fleeing pair.

* * *

Kathy Malz opened her front door to find the man she had mistaken for Karl, Stefan Krumholz, standing on her welcome mat.

"I had a few questions about… the estate," he said. Kathy invited him inside and closed the door.

* * *

Thank God for GPS, Jessica thought. It had come as a standard feature on the rental; they could see themselves nearing their destination. Although the immediate situation gave them a moment of relief, they both knew it was only temporary.

6

LONDON

Red-faced with veins popping from his forehead, the self-proclaimed Royal Excellency Wulf Xavier Johan III, head of the New Order of the Holy Roman Empire (NOHRE), screamed, "What? The records are *missing*?"

Although they had duplicates on the computer's hard drive and elsewhere, the originals had information that, in the wrong hands, could ruin their master plan.

"That egotistical bastard," his predecessor, HRE Wilhelm von Battenberg fumed, referring to Henry Conrad. "We should have let them finish him off long ago when we had the chance."

Wulf was a grisly, shrunken man. Although the years had not been kind to him, his regal aura exuded from him even as he sat in the massive, overstuffed chair.

"Enough!" the current emperor commanded. "What's done is done. And now we *must* recover what they stole. We have stepped up the plans. Two centuries of waiting for world domination is about to be rewarded. This setback will only serve to remind us to be ever-cautious. Now that we've got our world leaders in place, it's time to make our move."

Unbeknownst to the current leaders all over the world, the

NOHRE had groomed either the leader himself or those immediately at the right hand of power to make decisions based on the basic humanistic premises that the NOHRE proclaimed. They were patient and insidious, giving the appearance of morality with their humanitarian facade, but with the underlying path of eliminating the unperfect, the unclean. Their minions had a strong aversion to Israel and were strong on socialist programs, slowly putting government controls over aspects of the public's lives so when the time came, the elimination of those who were not "the fittest" would be morally accepted as a good thing. The world was their puppet, and NOHRE pulled the strings; whether by collusion or serendipity, they cared not, for the timing of their rise was at hand.

"We will *prevail!*" His voice reached a crescendo, slamming his fist on the table.

7

NEW YORK CITY

The Rabbinical Jews in the room were the majority, with scattered others in business suits.

"Thank you for arriving on such a short notice, but I trust you will find the information I'm about to convey to be worth the inconvenience. As you know, we occasionally receive random calls from an individual or family member with articles of questionable origins that they want to donate to the Archives. As in the case of the elderly soldier who brought us ancient manuscripts taken as a souvenir from the Merkers' Mine, we have no way of knowing what is still out there and what we will never know was missing.

I have just received information about a cache of ledgers that the SS used to record information that we had heard rumors of existing but had no proof of. That is... until now."

Greg Simpson had their full attention.

"I believe that *if* this is what I think it is, it is one of the most important groups of documents we have ever seen. If the story of its provenance we were told is true, the source is impeccable, and its authenticity can easily be verified. This information comes to us by the grandson of the butcher we all knew as Reinhard Heydrich, who we believed to be assassinated in 1942."

The room resonated with low murmurs.

"We have contacts at the museums and banks, and they will send detailed information on the art and valuables that they have been holding since World War II, waiting for just such records to surface, not that they ever thought they would. The families who have filed lawsuits with attempts to recover items have mostly been dismissed for lack of evidence. If these records are what I think they are, they will be the missing link for final restitution.

"We all know that there has been recent evidence that the Nazi regime will try once again to come to power. They won't just sit back and let this evidence come to light. The grandson who is en route with the ledgers is being followed and may be in danger as we speak. We have them as protected as is possible right now, with escorts bringing them in, and they are under an hour away. Time is of the essence. So, I ask you and all your authority to assist in doing whatever it takes to keep these people and the documents safe. Billions of dollars of gold, jewelry, art, and valuables can finally go to their rightful homes."

Greg glanced at his watch. "I have to leave now. Be advised, I'll keep you posted."

* * *

The two businessmen and their female assistant asked to see the curator and were led to his office.

"Do you have an appointment?" asked the secretary.

"No, but I'm sure he'll want to see us."

She had a quick exchange via intercom with her boss. "Go on in."

"Thank you for seeing us in such short notice," the leader said as he shut the door, deftly locking it with his thumb. "There's something I wanted to show you."

He approached the director's desk. The last thing Greg remembered seeing was the unusual insignia on the man's ring on his right hand as he opened a small box. A quick rush toward his face with the box holding a cotton pad soaked in a foul chemical gave Greg little time to react before he passed out.

"Quickly, get him in the closet."

* * *

Karl and Jessica arrived at the National Archives main office; their escort paused before driving off. They followed the instructions Greg had given them to his office, knowing he'd be there waiting for them.

"Right this way, please." They were brought into the curator's office. *Division of written records* was on a plaque on the wall next to the door.

"Sir, they are here," the woman posing as the secretary announced as she let them into the office.

"Hello, glad to meet you." The "curator" stood up from the desk and extended his hand. "This is my assistant, Mr. Mossy." Another bulky figure of a man stood in the shadows of the room.

Mr. Mossy shot "Greg" a look as he shook Karl's and Jessica's hands. He didn't like the name his boss had just bestowed upon him.

"I'm Karl Conrad, and this is Jessica Sinclair."

"Yes, I'm glad you made it safely. Where are the ledgers?" Karl and Jessica mistook the anticipation in his voice for excitement. "We'll have to examine them closely to make sure they are the real thing."

"Well, I've brought one in for you to see," Karl said as he pulled the ledger from under his jacket and handed him the old book. The old grey ledger had a white rectangular block on the cover. Written in black ink, scrolled one word: *Auschwitz*.

The imposter known to Karl and Jessica as Greg had heard about these books, but to finally hold one... He snatched the ledger from Karl and briefly leafed through it.

"Where are the others?"

Jessica zeroed in on the ring he wore. She'd seen that emblem before but couldn't place it. Maybe on the internet in her searching... Something to do with the National Archives? Karl's words brought her back to the present.

"The rest of the books are downstairs. We'll need some help. There's quite a few boxes." "Mr. Moss, would you be so kind as to make the arrangements?" He nodded solemnly and left the room.

Jessica, knowing from her real estate business the importance of remembering names, caught the error — hadn't "Greg" introduced him as "Mr. Mossy?"

And then she remembered where she had seen the insignia on the ring.

"Karl," Jessica said sharply, speaking for the first time, giving Karl a look the others couldn't see, cutting her eyes to the door, "let's show them where we parked."

Karl could tell something had agitated Jessica, but she was suggesting something out of their agreed upon protocol. Prior to arriving, Karl and Jessica had discussed their strategy — to sit down and discuss at length with Greg what was the best scenario, before any boxes were unloaded. He knew something was up. Her eyes were darting around the room to the photos on the wall.

"Nice office," she said, strolling around the perimeter of the room. Jessica looked at the array of photos, with one man included over and over in the photos who was *not* the Greg they had just met.

Karl, realizing they may be in somewhat of a pickle, waited for his chance and winked at Jessica. "Well, let's go down, and I'll show you exactly where the rest of the ledgers are," Karl offered and headed for the door.

"Very well, my assistant will accompany you," Greg said as they exited the office, referring to the bulky man from the shadows in the rear. As soon as they departed, he made a phone call. "We have them."

Leaving the office, Jessica noticed the nameplate on the secretary's desk. Addressing the secretary who was down the hallway near the elevator with her back to them, she said, "Miss Andrews?", which did not elicit a response from the woman. Jessica tried again, a bit louder. "Miss Andrews?" The "secretary" finally realized Jessica was addressing her and suddenly turned around and walked back toward them.

"Yes?"

"I just wanted to thank you for helping us so much when we called earlier," Jessica lied. "Oh, yes, of course. Always glad to be of assistance," she replied, returning to her desk, confirming Jessica's suspicions and giving Karl the knowledge that something was definitely amiss.

When they had originally called, the secretary had been at lunch, and the curator himself had answered the phone. They had never spoken to her.

Karl and Jessica walked shoulder to shoulder, with the goon in step behind them. After trying to convey a nonverbal message to each other under the goon's watchful eye, Jessica dropped back and took their escort's arm.

"I have a question for you..." Jessica began, giving Karl the opportunity to drop back also to walk on his other side. They reached the closed elevator doors and noticed the floor indicator was at the lowest level. Karl pushed the down button and gave a slight nod to Jessica.

Jessica stomped on the man's foot, coming down hard with her heel on the center of his foot, jabbing her elbow into his jaw as he doubled over, then she kneed him hard in the groin. For any normal man, this sudden attack would have left him powerless. Unfortunately, he was well trained, angry, and poised to retaliate as quickly as his reflexes would allow him to. Karl quickly stepped in with a solid strike to his cheek, then windpipe, knocking him out cold.

They stood there a second, looking at each other in shock. Then they dragged him into the nearby stairwell and returned to the elevator just in time for the doors to open, only to find themselves face to face with Mr. Moss, or Mossy, or whoever the hell he was.

"Hey, your boss wants to see you. We're bringing the car around," Karl quipped. "Uh, okay," he said, and as he exited, they entered, quickly pushing the button. The doors began to shut, and they could hear him saying something as the unlikeliness of their leaving unescorted dawned on him. "Hey, wait a minute..."

The doors shut, and they began the slowest descent, down to the parking garage level.

"We only have a few minutes before they realize what's going on," Karl stated.

They bolted out of the elevator, nearly bowling over an elderly woman with a large bag. Karl apologized as they ran full speed to the car.

The car doors chirped, unlocked from the remote key just as Karl and Jessica reached the vehicle. They jumped in and took off, burning rubber, speeding toward the exit. They slowed down at the gate, calmly paid their fee, and even before the barrier was completely raised, they took off again like a bat out of hell.

"What just happened?" Karl prompted Jessica.

"His ring. It had the insignia of the Holy Roman Empire. An eagle with two heads. There's no way the real Greg Simpson would have had that. Then I noticed that the guy in all the photos wasn't the guy behind the desk."

Karl added, "His voice — completely different than on the phone. Plus, I expected a far different reaction when I gave him the Auschwitz ledger. When we looked at it, we were almost sick because of the atrocities tied to that death camp. This guy was almost ecstatic. Then the bogus secretary... Makes me wonder what happened to the people who were supposed to be there..." His voice trailed off.

He wondered if they were okay. He had put their lives at risk just by contacting them, which meant they needed to be more careful about involving others. What kind of mess had they gotten themselves into?

"And you... You were awesome. Where did you learn those moves?" he asked, forcing himself to shelve those thoughts for now, astonished at Jessica's action.

"Well," Jessica began, "when you are a woman realtor who meets strangers in houses for a living, sometimes at night, sometimes in secluded areas, you've got to be prepared to defend yourself. Not that I've ever needed to use it before. But I'm glad my broker insisted our agents took those self-defense classes. A little Taekwondo never hurt anybody. Well, I guess Mr. Poser back there would disagree. And what about you? You came to my rescue pretty quickly and took him out. You knocked him unconscious."

"Yeah, well, grandpa's boxing lessons were finally put to good use," Karl replied as he pulled into a parking garage. "Let's regroup. There's a diner across the street from here. I'm starving, so let's park where we can watch the car. No one knows us around here, so we're safe to sit, have a bite to eat, and decide what to do next."

They brought Jessica's laptop into the greasy-spoon diner, sunk into the deeply padded seats of the booth, and ordered the special of the day: layered meatloaf on a slice of white bread with potatoes, and drowned in brown gravy.

"Now where?" Jessica asked, "We can't go back to the National Archives… But the bigger question I have is, why do they want to stop us so badly? Connecting survivor's families with their valuables sitting in limbo in vaults couldn't possibly cause that kind of response. What else is there that these books reveal?"

The waitress delivered her plate.

"Mm, I've never smelled anything more delicious," she said, digging into the mountain of food.

"Well," Karl said with food in his mouth, swallowed, and continued, "we have inventories of cities, concentration camps, and the castles and caves that these items were stored in. There's a master list of the ledgers that I compiled when you were sleeping the other night. I put it in the pocket of your briefcase."

Jessica stopped mid-chew and scowled.

"What? I thought it would be a safe place to keep it," Karl explained.

"What else have you done while I was sleeping that you haven't told me?" Asked Jessica.

Karl laughed loudly, causing the occupants of the sparsely populated diner to look in their direction.

"Yeah, look who's talking. I still want to know why you hid those ledgers. Thief!" Karl replied.

"Okay, fine. It's a long story." Jessica pushed her dish away.

"I'm not going anywhere," Karl said with conviction.

"My grandfather came from this city," she said as she removed the ledger marked *Bratislava*. "He was at this concentration camp." She pulled out the other ledger, marked *Theresienstadt*. "His name was Daniel Sinclair. Grandma always told the story about how God reached His hand down and saved Grandpa from the fate of the others. He came from an important family and was wealthy. They had several homes, one on a lake in Austria. Because of his connections there, he was named as one of the 1,200 Jewish prisoners "bought" out of Terezin by Austrian sympathizers just before the Allies arrived. His other family members were already dead. My grandfather never spoke of it to me, but he did say he would not have been around if he hadn't been bought and paid for, and neither would I. He carried a good bit of guilt that he was spared while so many others that he knew had died.

"This happened just before the Allies arrived. When the Allies were getting close to freeing the camp, the Nazis marched most of the remaining prisoners cross-country to load them on barges with the intention of sinking them to hide any traces that they existed. But because they were so weak from starvation, disease, and malnutrition, most died on the march, and very few survived. The Allies arrived before they made it to the barges. I heard this story only once — Grandpa had been drinking, and I overheard him telling someone when I was a little girl. I was hiding around the corner, so he never knew.

"My granny escaped before the craziness began, but she lost almost all her friends and family to the camps. Her parents sent her away to boarding school in England where she would be safe just before the restrictions began. My granny never completely recovered from losing everyone. She told me that even when she was in England, she had dreams, more like nightmares, of those she lost crying for help. They've never stopped. After Grandpa died, she got worse — cries all the time... She's in a nursing home now."

Jessica's words drifted off, and she inhaled deeply. She looked out the plate glass window at the sea of businessmen, ladies with shopping bags, and teenagers without a care in the world passing by, blissfully unaware that there were horrible things that had happened to so many in other parts of the world. She gathered her thoughts and began again.

"Anyway, I found Grandpa's name in the Bratislava ledger. They listed the paintings, jewelry, silver menorahs — stuff like that. It's a long list of what they took from his house. It's right here." Jessica opened the page she had bookmarked. "By the time he got to Terezin, he only had a watch and a ring." She pointed to the entry in the ledger for *Theresienstadt* under *Daniel Sinclair, Bratislava*.

Karl was silent. Watching her disclose this information so seemingly nonchalantly was unnerving, but her glistening eyes betrayed her.

"Thank you," Karl said, gently touching her hand. "I know that must have been difficult to talk about." Now he knew the reason for some of her odd behavior. He also realized that they both had reasons deep within their souls that cried out for restitution for past sins.

"Before we turn over the ledgers, we need to copy the pages that pertain to your grandfather. But once that's done, we've got to decide where we go from here," Karl said as Jessica attempted to eat her lunch.

When finished, Jessica opened her laptop to search the internet.

"The Simon Wiesenthal Museum of Tolerance may be a good place," Jessica suggested, hesitating for a moment, "but how did they know we were going to the National Archives? By tracing who we called from our cell phones? Maybe we shouldn't use our phones and should be vaguer about why we want to meet. It sounds paranoid, but I think we've underestimated them so far. Since the Simon Weisenthal group has people tracking down the Nazis that escaped in the Ratlines, I bet they have their phones bugged, too. What do you think?"

"Sounds like a plan. Let's go." Karl stood up, leaving plenty of cash on the table to cover their lunch, plus a generous tip.

8

AUSTRIA

"Idiot," Hans Sprechter growled into the phone and slammed it down on the table. If only he were forty years younger, he'd handle this himself. Mumbling profanities in German under his breath, he slowly made his way down the great hall. Portraits of nobility lined the walls of the corridor, which seemed to continue forever, the end hidden in the dim lighting. The murals spanning the arched ceiling were illuminated, coming to life as light from incandescent lamps wired to motion sensors were triggered by his slow march. He cursed his old bones, angry that his body was fading when his mind was still sharp; and now especially so, since he was about to realize his life's work. He was surer than ever that his investment in cryogenics would not be a waste. But right now, he craved the solace of his favorite room.

He swung open the double doors of his study, a two-story library with bookshelves lining the four walls, tall ladders on rolling tracks to reach the top shelves, and a balcony to reach the uppermost. He hadn't been on the balcony for years; his knees could no longer take the strain of the spiral staircase.

Typically, he would sit in his favorite leather wingback chair by the fireplace and make his plans while nursing a brandy. Today, however, he made a beeline for the far back corner of the room. Pulling the corners of several old volumes halfway out of their resting place on the shelf, he heard the old familiar click. The section of books silently swung open. Entering the doorway, he maneuvered down the old stone steps of the narrow passageway, grasping the old rope banister, finally arriving at the bottom into a large, secure room that had been carved out of the same stone that the castle's foundation rested on. State-of-the-art computers and maps filled the room, and about twenty personnel were concentrating on their specific tasks. A few did a double take as they noticed the ancient patriarch; rarely did he grace them with his presence.

"I need to talk to you... *now*," Hans wheezed. Typically, his requests, or rather, demands, received immediate attention anyway, but his sharp tone indicated that *now* wasn't soon enough.

His first in command followed him into the next room. The stone bedrock room made for natural soundproofing. As much as his subordinates revered Hans Sprechter, there were those who saw his obvious signs of weakness: his aging body, his increased lack of reason, his failing health. If he faltered at all, there would be others fighting like a pack of hyenas over his command. They smelled the blood of a wounded brother and were hovering over the kill. His era as commander in chief was nearing an end.

"You have failed — *again*," the red-faced octogenarian began. "This ineptness cannot — no, *will* not — be tolerated. How hard is it to find this man? How is the woman connected to this? Why can't your trained hunting dogs track down two civilians? How hard can it be? How *stupid* are you people?"

Hans Sprechter's veins popped out, visible rivers on his forehead and neck.

Nathanial Schultz knew from experience that it was best to let the old warrior get it all out of his system before attempting to appease him. The sad thing was, he agreed with the old man and was just as bewildered as to why his team had not had the desired result. The team's record had, until now, been stellar. They completed their missions with no trace of their involvement; their typical covers being random gangland robberies, muggings, car accidents, or accidental drownings. It was possible his men were becoming complacent, slacking off, and losing sight of their goal. Maybe they just got sloppy, thinking this time would be easy since they weren't dealing with an equally trained adversary who, by nature, would be sleeping with one eye open and constantly looking over his shoulder, aware of potential danger. It should have been a slam dunk. "Could their targets be more involved and experienced than they had thought? Were they tied to any of the various organizations that had been trying for decades to stop them? For centuries?

Nathanial decided the only logical explanation was that they must be tied to one of those very groups that had been a thorn in their side throughout the course of the Holy Roman Empire's history. How else could they have the means to overcome his highly trained associates?

Ha! They think they can outwit us — but the reality is they will fall like the others, he concluded to himself.

With a newfound confidence, Nathanial addressed his mentor. "There is a good reason they have eluded us. They are better connected than we thought. We will not underestimate them again. I know our operatives failed, and they will suffer the consequences, but now that we know who we are dealing with, we will crush them." *Or, they had better*, he thought. His own reputation was on the line, and he would *not* allow the fallacies of others put that in danger.

Hans Sprechter had calmed down a little, the effects of the adrenaline still evident. He was still completely frustrated with this new generation of inadequate imbeciles and would have thrashed them himself if he had the strength. But for now, he needed to sit down, wishing he could take a deep breath of oxygen from the tank he kept hidden in his room.

"I don't believe you fully realize what is happening here. If the documents they have get into the wrong hands, our plan will not only be found out, but the caches not yet found, that were hidden by the Fuhrer to fund the Fourth Reich, would be plundered. This information can *not* be in the wrong hands." Herr Sprechter was turning red again.

"I will handle it." Nathanial had realized the critical nature of the task but was also losing his patience and temper with the old man. Being rebuked had never sat well with him, even as a young boy. One schoolteacher who had humiliated him ended up gravely ill soon after; no one had ever suspected him. As an adult, the distaste of being reprimanded was even stronger.

He left Hans Sprechter, went to his private office, and made a phone call.

* * *

Karl and Jessica had two hours until they would reach the Simon Wiesenthal Museum of Tolerance. No one seemed to be following them this time. Jessica had emailed the foundation from her laptop, picking up unsecured Wi-Fi at one of their stops. She had explained what they had in their possession and their intentions. They had arranged a meeting for the next morning, which meant one more night on the lam.

By cutting off their communication, they had been able to stay under the radar from their pursuers and allowed for plenty of time to exchange their life stories.

Jessica had grown up as a non-functioning Jew, recognizing the most important holidays — Hanukkah, Rosh Hashanah, Passover. But the religion she inherited had not been an active part of her life. Her grandparents were the only link she had to her heritage. Daniel and Lorene had met after the war, their unspoken grief a strong bond. Theirs was a love fiercer than any other couple she had known. When one cried, the other tasted salt.

A few years ago, when her grandfather died of a stroke, her poor granny was at a loss. After losing so many friends and family during the war, Grandpa was her everything. Once he was gone, she was an empty shell, waiting for the day she would join him once again, beyond the Pearly Gates. She became more delusional, claiming to be visited by those that had died in her past. Jessica's family believed this because of all the medications she was on. Her downward spiral had been slowly coming to an end.

Jessica's parents had passed away long ago to cancer, only two years apart. The doctors insisted there wasn't a correlation to their illnesses, but both had grown up in Minnesota farming communities of the 1940s and 1950s when dangerous chemicals were routinely used. They used to dump lead into the white paint and thought the fire protection that asbestos provided was the next best thing to sliced bread.

They remembered the radiation machines that were in the drug stores that would cure just about anything. Jessica also suspected the vitamin kick her mom went on when Jessica was in high school, taking five to ten different vitamins at every meal, even those that could cause toxic buildup in the body, like vitamin A. Cancer wasn't all that surprising.

So, Jessica was proactive about her health, doing whatever she believed to be right; not microwaving plastics, avoiding eating products that were bio-engineered or had added hormones. Knowing that one day, despite her best efforts, some of her "healthy" habits might also be found to be detrimental to her health, Jessica had a personal motto to live each day to its fullest... just in case.

As Karl and Jessica drove, Jessica shared how she had married young, assuming the solid unconditional love exhibited by her grandparents to be the norm, only to find out the harsh reality of "marital bliss." Her hasty decision to marry Chuck resulted in years of unhappiness. Their lives were busy; each involved in their own interests and not each other's. They eventually grew apart and ended up as strangers sharing the same roof. Both were relieved when they decided on a trial separation, then divorce. As much as she had never thought she would divorce, Jessica felt like a bird let out of a cage, and happiness returned to her life. She vowed never to lose her independence again, believing incorrectly that a relationship meant defeat. Her life post-divorce was satisfying, and she wouldn't trade it for the world.

Jessica had been divorced for several years now but had not dated anyone seriously since the failure of her marriage. She had become accustomed to doing whatever she wanted to do whenever she wanted to do it.

At first, she wasn't interested in the men who attempted to woo her. Eventually, the offers dwindled as it became evident that she just wasn't interested. She had decided to be a bit more discerning after the fiasco of her fifteen-year marriage, not wishing to settle, and decided her newfound independence suited her. Now she had plenty of free time to throw herself into what she loved most — her work. As a result, she had excelled at being a realtor, known for her "matchmaking" skills — finding the perfect home for her clients. Her success was rewarding to her, having come up the ranks from novice to one of the top agents in her firm over the past few years.

Karl, on the other hand, had dated often and had many lovers but would not let anyone get close enough to know his heart. His only personal reference for a healthy, loving relationship had been that of his parents, but since distancing himself from them with the help of his grandfather, he viewed their bond as a weakness. The only time he had let his guard down long enough to allow someone in was when he dated Rachel.

* * *

The sun was sinking when they finally made it to Manhattan. They drove past the Simon Wiesenthal Museum of Tolerance, a bit hesitant after their experience at the National Archives, checking out the parking situation and the accessibility of the building. On the next block, Karl found a hotel.

The Tudor provided a place until their morning meeting. They parked in the garage next door, took out their overnight bags, and made sure everything else was covered from view. They noted the security cameras and the extra security guards stationed at intervals in the garage, which allowed Karl and Jessica to leave their treasure with confidence.

"I'd like a suite with two bedrooms for tonight, please," Karl told the front desk.

"I'm sorry, sir, we only have one room available tonight. It does have a Queen bed and a couch. Will that do?" The little nameplate over her left breast pocket said *Annette*.

Karl looked at Jessica. "We can try somewhere else—" Karl began.

"Are you kidding me? No way am I driving around anymore. This is close to where we need to be in the morning, and we've already locked up the car." Jessica headed for the elevator. "I just want to crash somewhere — anywhere. I don't care."

"You heard the lady. We'll take it." Karl finished the paperwork and met Jessica at the elevator with the keys.

Jessica pulled back the drapes in the spacious room. Their fourth-floor view let them admire the lights of Manhattan. There was an anonymity of being just another guest that embraced them. Karl found the remote, switched the news on, then grabbed the ice bucket.

"I'm going for ice. It's just down the hall by the elevator. I'll be right back."

"Want some coffee?" Jessica asked, taking the coffee pot to the sink.

"No, not for me. Any caffeine at this hour will keep me up," Karl replied.

"Not me. I've always been a little hyper, so coffee actually makes me tired," Jessica replied as Karl left the room.

As the water from the bathroom sink filled up the coffee pot, Jessica thought she heard a familiar name on the television. Turning the water off, she made a beeline for the remote on the coffee table and cranked up the volume.

"Kathy Malz, who had been missing since yesterday, was discovered this morning, dead, in a rock quarry just outside the Kansas City metro area. It appears that she was tortured, then shot execution style with her hands tied behind her back. Forensic reports will indicate the exact cause of death."

Karl had returned with the ice and gravitated over to the television.

"A note with the inscription, 'You know what we want,' was found next to her body. Anyone with any information is asked to call the Kansas Bureau of Investigation or the Tips Hotline."

"Wow, that poor woman..." Karl began, his voice trailing off as soon as he caught a glimpse of Jessica's pale face, frozen in shock.

"Did you know her?" he asked.

"It's Kathy," she whispered. "She is... was... the person handling your estate sale." Jessica locked eyes with Karl. "That message, 'You know what we want' — that's for us. My God, what are these people capable of?" she exclaimed angrily.

"It's my fault... I never should have involved Kathy. If only I hadn't called her, she would be alive right now." Guilt crept into Jessica's voice as she clumsily sat, almost missing the edge of the couch.

Karl shook his head. "You are not responsible whatsoever for her death. If anyone's to blame, it's me. I'm the one who wanted you to arrange for an estate sale. Neither of us knew what we were getting into, and if we did it all over again, my guess is that we'd make the same decisions."

He had moved over to Jessica and knelt down, taking her by the shoulders, and forced her to look into his eyes. "The people who are after us are nutcases. That could have easily been us, and we need to be thankful we're still around. I'm very sorry for your friend, but don't blame yourself. We are dealing with people with no morals or decency. This is their way of sending us a message to let us know they mean business, that's all."

Karl racked his brain, wondering if they had put anyone else in harm's way without realizing it; how careless had he been? He thought of the people they were to meet tomorrow at the Museum of Tolerance. *They already know what kind of monsters these people were... are.*

Jessica's tears quietly came, slow and hesitant at first but gathering steam as the cumulative effects of the past few days took their toll. Soon, her body wracked with uncontrollable sobs.

Karl hated when women cried. Feeling helpless, he did the only thing he could think of. He pulled her up from the couch and wrapped her in his arms and allowed her to let it all out. His physical support made Jessica melt in his arms as she let herself accept the warm protection and strength of his embrace.

Her hair had an earthy smell, faintly reminiscent of strawberries. Karl inhaled a deep breath as he stroked Jessica's hair, his lips occasionally brushing the top of her head.

"It's okay," he whispered in her ear. "Just let it all out…"

He could feel Jessica's body relax as her weeping gave way to intermittent sobs, broken by hiccupped gasps as the grief subsided. She had her head resting heavily on his shoulder, quiet now, with only an occasional shudder and sniff.

Jessica could feel that their bodies had pressed themselves hard against each other. Part of her told herself not to like this so much and to pull away, but the stronger part of her liked it and would not permit her to disengage.

Karl, thankful the crying had stopped, found himself strangely content to have Jessica secure and safe in his arms. He continued to gently stroke her hair and rub her back. He felt his hand press on her back, drawing Jessica even closer to him, feeling the warmth of her chest tight against his. Karl's other hand caressed the small of her back. He felt her arms slide up his back to his shoulders as the embrace was returned.

Karl's hands slowly made their way up her back, neck, and he took her head in both hands to tilt her face up toward his. He gazed down and lost himself in her hazel eyes, gently brushing the last tears from her cheek.

Jessica sniffed and looked directly into his soul through his sea-blue eyes.

Karl cupped her face in his hands and drew his lips toward hers. He brushed her lips with his, kissing her slowly, sweetly, gaining confidence. They drew apart, eyes still locked, and after only a moment's hesitation, came together again with mutual fervor, his tongue parting her lips.

The stress, anxiety, and adrenaline of the past few days created a tinderbox of passion. Jessica couldn't get close enough to his body, desperately wanting to feel his skin against hers. In a passionate frenzy, they clawed at each other's buttons and zippers.

Still intertwined, they stumbled toward the bed, kicking off their shoes. Karl lifted Jessica's shirt over her head, pulling her almost-naked body against his, the electric power of their bodies colliding, sending sparks flying.

They fell onto the bed, kissing urgently, throwing off the last articles of clothing. The first time they made love was fast and furious. The rest of the night's lovemaking was slower; they relished each moment as they explored every nuance of each other's bodies.

They didn't sleep for hours, repeating their passion as often as they could, finally falling into a deep sleep out of sheer exhaustion, spent and fully satisfied.

* * *

They were naked. Everyone was. The huge gates opened. *To each his own*, the letters on the gate's sign heralded, and she entered. But she wasn't Jessica anymore. She was a man in uniform; a soldier being cheered on and welcomed as he walked through the gates. Standing everywhere were naked skeleton-people, having hardly enough skin to draw over their bones, eyes hollow and sunken with gaunt cheekbones.

Their hands reached out toward her. They tried to put her on their shoulders like a hero but were too weak. Another door opened to a barracks. Inside were rows upon rows of bunk beds stacked floor to ceiling with only enough space above each for someone to lie down. The stench was overwhelming; every skin-stretched skull turned to look at her. They were too weak to stand, but their haunting eyes pierced her as she passed row after row of naked men in their bunks. Then the bunks were gone. In their place were piles of dead bodies, stacked like cords of wood against the building. A large black crow landed, frightening her, making her jump with its loud caw.

Jessica sat bolt-upright in the bed. As the swirling darkness settled, she heard it again. The phone. Clumsily grasping the receiver, she mumbled, "Hello?"

"Front Desk with your wake-up call. Have a great day," she heard. "Uhnngh," she replied.

What kind of sadistic person would be that cheerful at the crack of dawn? She rolled over and came face to face with a sleeping Karl, initially startling her. The passion of the previous night came flooding back. No matter what today brought, she had a happiness inside that made her glow from the inside out. How nice it would have been to just be lazy today and rely on room service. She watched him sleep for a moment.

"Thank you, God, for unexpected gifts," she prayed for the first time in years, then woke Karl up in the best possible way.

After jostling around again, Karl rolled over, satisfied. "Good morning," he said.

"Mm, it is." Jessica kissed him and slid out of bed. "I definitely need a shower."

"Yes, you do," Karl teased. "That sounds good." He followed her. "Do you mind washing my back?"

"My pleasure."

* * *

They had planned to walk the block to the Museum of Tolerance, carrying only a few of the ledgers in Jessica's briefcase. Their meeting was at 9:00 am. Anxiety fueled their walk. Since they did not call to announce this visit, the pair felt confident that this time there would be no surprises.

The pair found their destination in minutes and were led into a room of shelves holding rows of boxes as far as the eye could see. They were brought to a table, asked to sit, and were joined by a member of the society.

"It is my extreme pleasure to meet you." The gentleman in the brown suit and bow tie said. "I'm Bernard Hughes, curator of... let's say... *special items*... and I'm very intrigued to see what you have found. I apologize for being so direct, but may I have a look?"

"Of course." Jessica removed the ledgers from her briefcase.

Mr. Hughes took a pair of cotton gloves from his drawer and gently took the books from her. With an almost loving quality, he scoured the pages. A tear formed in the corner of his eye. With an occasional "Hm" or "Ah," Mr. Hughes immersed himself in the manuscripts. The precise notations of names, addresses, and inventory by the Nazi SS reduced thousands of individuals' anguish into a neat, tidy inventory of horror.

After perusing the books for several minutes, Mr. Hughes quietly closed the cover of the last one and set the books aside.

"Yes, these are authentic. It grieves me to no end to handle the same books that the instigators of such pain have created." He sighed. "But in the end, we will use these for restitution — to make some good come out of all that evil, to return the gold, jewelry, artwork, and more to those who have suffered at their hands. That is, if there are any descendants left."

Karl's voice faltered. "I cannot express to you how much I wish to correct in any small way the harm my grandfather and his cohorts have done. Putting these records into your hands is the very least I can do."

Jessica reached over and touched his arm.

"Please know that although my grandfather's blood runs through my veins, I am *not* him and will never comprehend how he saw his heinous acts as good."

Mr. Hughes nodded, his eyes filled with compassion. "These sins are not yours. God bless you now for sharing this information." He put a comforting hand on Karl's shoulder.

Jessica, remembering the list they made of the ledgers, scrounged her briefcase until she produced his copy.

"Here. We wrote the names on the front of each book that we have with us," she told him, handing the papers over to him.

Mr. Hughes took the list, scanning it. The list consisted of the names of all the cities dissidents and Jews were taken from, and of each concentration or death camp. Then there were ledgers for the caves, castles, storage units, banks, and places the confiscated items were hidden.

The excitement of the day and the multiple cups of coffee Jessica drank that morning finally caught up with her.

"I'm sorry, but is there a restroom I could use?" she asked.

"Of course. Just out this door, down the corridor to your left." Mr. Hughes indicated, not looking up, engrossed in the list.

"Excuse me," Jessica said reluctantly, not wanting to miss a moment of the meeting. "I've got a bladder the size of a pea."

Determined to relieve herself quickly and return to the room, she scurried down the hall. She didn't notice the tall gentleman engrossed in the postings on the hall's bulletin board. As she entered the bathroom, he glanced down both sides of the empty hallway, then followed her in.

Mr. Hughes was still reviewing the list. He jerked. Karl, who had been patiently watching him, saw his expression change to perplexity.

"Hm..." Mr. Hughes took a pen and paper and jotted down several place names from the list, names not familiar to him. He picked up the phone's receiver on the table and dialed his secretary. "Helen, would you please look up these places on our database?" He proceeded to read off four or five place names. "Tell me what information we have about those locations."

"What is it?" Karl asked, noting the concerned look on Mr. Hughes' face.

Mr. Hughes put the call on speaker and addressed Karl. "I am familiar with every town, village, and city that the Nazi's controlled. I know of every camp and location they hid their stolen goods. But on your lists, I see names of places I've never heard of. It's very perplexing."

The secretary's voice over speaker phone interrupted them. "I'm sorry, sir, but those names are not in the database."

Mr. Hughes looked at Karl. After a couple of minutes, Karl broke the silence. "So, does that mean they never found all of Hitler's hiding places?"

"Possibly." Mr. Hughes got up and walked over to one of the shelves and took out a map of Europe. He found the names of the locations on the map. "This map is from the time of the war. See here? Each of those places is either a mine or a cave, which have consistent temperatures. Here is a castle built hundreds of years ago to be a fortress. Each is next to a major rail line or highway for ease of transport. But to move anything major after the Nazis fell out of power would be too conspicuous. If that is the case, and these strongholds hid stolen treasure, it would have been almost impossible to remove it after the Allies took over."

"Well, surely it's not still there," Karl said, trying to comprehend it. "And if it is still there, why would they leave it? I'd have figured a way to get it out of there, even a little at a time... Unless..." Karl trailed off as he remembered some of his grandfather's letter that he found in the safety deposit box.

"What?" Mr. Hughes studied Karl. "Unless what?"

"When my grandfather died, there were some papers for me in the safety deposit box in his bank. There may be a lot more to this than I had originally thought. Which would explain why they've been so desperate to stop us."

A knot was forming in the pit of Karl's stomach.

"From what he wrote, there are plans to restore the Holy Roman Empire — to create a Fourth Reich... and he did say they had a way to fund it. I wonder if they planned to take over those countries again to access the treasure, if it's indeed still there, to pay for their movement. If it was still all hidden, it would be worth billions in today's market..."

Karl realized Jessica had been a long time. "What time was it when Jessica left?"

Mr. Hughes looked at his watch. "It's been half an hour."

Karl jumped up and ran down the hall to the women's bathroom. "Jessica," he shouted into the room. No answer. He hesitated only a moment before bursting into the room, scaring the lone occupant washing her hands at the sink, making her shriek.

Ignoring her, Karl pounded on the stall doors, yelling, "Jessica," his voice laced with panic. His blood ran cold as he noticed one of her shoes pushed up against the wall behind the door as it shut after the frazzled woman's hasty exit. Mr. Hughes, panting and not used to running, entered the restroom to find an angry Karl.

"They've got her."

* * *

Light, then dark. Light, then dark. She was aware of a rocking — back and forth, side to side as the rhythmic sound of the railroad tracks thundered in her ears. She cracked open an eye and found a small child with huge, forlorn eyes staring at her. The stench was atrocious; a combination of feces, sweat, gaseous emissions, body odor, vomit, and smoke filled the metal compartment they travelled in. She couldn't move — too many people packed into too small a space.

The wide eyes of the little boy locked on her, both rocked by the swaying of the boxcar.

"Help me." She could see him mouth the words, but no sound came out. The noise and the pounding in her skull increased to the point where she thought her head would explode. The cigar smell made bile swell up her esophagus. The darkness slowly began to fade as she felt someone pick her up. She tried to move but was paralyzed. She recognized the voice as the guard from the concentration camp who had shown her the lampshade.

"Here we are, my pretty."

* * *

"Bring her in here."

She had initially put up a good fight, and left scratches on him to prove it, but this time, they'd been prepared. Chloroform worked wonders.

The years of monitoring the activities of the Museum of Tolerance had finally paid off. All their operatives had been alerted to be on the lookout for Karl and Jessica, and they had moved as soon as the report came in.

She was just waking up. They were curious to know her role in the theft of their property, and also who she worked for.

"Ah, Miss Sinclair," Stefan Krumholz said as she slowly came out of the drug's influence, trying in vain to resist the restraints. She squinted at the bright light, seeing nothing else. Her arms and legs were bound to the chair. "It's no use trying to free yourself."

Jessica couldn't see him but heard his footsteps echo as he walked around the perimeter of the room, in the shadows. A knot of panic began to crawl up her throat. Still groggy, she tried to speak and failed.

"Patience, my dear. The drug will fade in time."

She could now feel his hand brush her hair as he walked behind her, causing her skin to prickle and the hairs on the back of her neck stand up.

"You have given us quite a run for our money. That wasn't very nice of you."

He stroked her hair. Jessica, repelled by his touch, tried in vain to evade it. Suddenly, he grabbed a clump of her hair in his hand and pulled her head back, so she was looking at the ceiling lights. He brought his face over hers, blocking out the light, and she finally saw her captor. His crooked nose, his eyes — a startlingly clear blue; cold and calculating — his short-cropped hair, his breath reeking of cigar smoke.

"Well, well, you are finally awake. I hope you are ready to cooperate." He took a deep breath, inhaling her scent. He loosened his grasp on her hair, letting his fingers move slowly from the back to the front of her neck, cupping her chin, forcing her to maintain her upward gaze. The adrenaline flooding her system made the panic transform into fury. She thrashed her head and body, then spat in his face, causing him to release her in his surprise.

"Let me go," Jessica snarled.

"Bitch," he said, wiping her saliva off his face then slapping her across the cheek, leaving a bright red mark. "You will regret that."

The sting of his strike burned her eyes, making them well up with tears. The pain seared through her cheekbone, clearing her head and shaking the last bit of grogginess out of her system. She inhaled sharply, the dank, stagnant air filling her lungs.

Ugh. Cigar. She coughed as the smoke caught in her throat. Reining in her anger, she decided to play it smart; maybe she'd find a chink in their armor.

"Listen, I'm not sure why I'm here. What exactly do you want?" Jessica asked.

"What do I want? *What do I want*? Really? Do you think I'm stupid? You *know* what I want. Now, where is it?" He had already lost his patience with her, his short fuse lit and burnt.

"No. Honestly, I don't exactly know—" Her words were cut short as Stefan slapped her across her face again.

"Ow! Stop that. Just tell me."

"You bitch! You have stolen something that is not yours, driven across the country, and you say you *do not know*? Liar!" Stefan was about to slap her again.

"Wait. What do you want? The books? The art? What? But why? What good are they to you? They can't be worth that much."

Stefan halted mid slap.

"Ah. So you *do* know what I am talking about..." He stood behind her again and pulled her hair back from her shoulders, then caressed her neck. "It's *so* much better when you play along. We can do this easy or hard. Frankly I don't care which."

He let his hands move slowly down her neck to her collar bone. "Your skin — it is very soft," Stefan whispered in her ear.

His hands were moving slowly down toward her breasts. Jessica's repulsion was evident.

"Are you ready to play nice? Your friend— Kathy, was it? She didn't want to play at all..."

Jessica's eyes grew round with fear, and she couldn't breathe. She nodded that she would comply.

"Good. Cooperate with me, and maybe Kathy's children won't need a visit from their Uncle Stefan."

His hands stopped just shy of her breasts. He moved them back up around her neck, tightening slightly. Jessica's eyes widened as the air was blocked and he slowly loosened his grasp.

Stefan came around to her front, pulling a chair from the shadows, and sat down face to face.

"Now... where are the books?"

Jessica was perplexed. Why did it matter so much that they took the ledgers or where they were now? What difference did it make if items stolen long ago were now inaccessible in vaults, sitting in limbo for the descendants of the owners to claim? No one could access them now, so what was the harm?

Couldn't be that. Must be something else. Unless... she thought. *Unless there was more information in those books than they thought... What had they gotten themselves into?*

She knew he wouldn't hesitate to kill her just like they killed Kathy. Jessica thought quickly — she had to make sure whatever she told them didn't jeopardize her value to them. If she told them what they wanted to hear, she knew they would kill her. She had to stay alive.

"I don't know where they are," she said, hoping her confidence wouldn't betray the true insecurity of the lie she just told. It didn't work.

"Liar!" Stefan screamed as he jumped to his feet and slapped her again. "Did you know that there are telltale signs — indicators, if you will — that your body reveals when you are lying? You would be foolish to lie to me again."

Stefan regained control, brushed off the front of his shirt, sat down, and made eye contact with Jessica. "Now, let's try this another way."

He put both his hands on her knees, eyes still on hers, and slowly ran his hands up her thighs.

"Miss Sinclair, may I call you Jessica? You are *not* in any position to be lying to me, are you?"

Jessica, repulsed by his touch, shook her head.

"Where are the books?"

"Move your hands one more inch, buddy, and you'll never know." Jessica couldn't help it; under no circumstance would she allow him to go there.

Stefan was amused. He could tell from her eyes that she wasn't lying this time. He stopped and reluctantly withdrew his hands. "Are you ready to cooperate?"

She nodded.

"All right then, let's hear what you have to tell me, and then I'll decide what happens next."

"All I can tell you is that we left the books in my rental car. You know the one — you followed it, remember? Who knows what Karl did with them now." She honestly didn't know what they would have done with the load since she had been abducted. "How long have I been here? Knowing Karl, he would have moved the rental car from where we had it just to be safe."

Thank you, God. That was brilliant. Jessica threw up another quick prayer. *Now, please keep me alive.*

Stefan could tell she was, indeed, telling the truth. "I'll be back," he said as he leaned over her, cupping her face in his hands and forcing a long, wet, kiss on her lips. "Mm, nice."

As he strode out of the light into the shadows, Jessica spat his taste from her mouth. A door slammed, and she heard the click of it being locked. She had to think quickly. As much as she struggled, the duct tape holding her hands together would not give, but she kept furiously working the binding around her wrists, steadily trying to loosen them just a little.

Stefan watched her struggle from the darkened next room through the one-way window Jessica was unable to see through. She amused him. It was refreshing to see a filly with some spunk; not at all like Kathy, who was hysterical and begged him to stop. He took no joy in such annoyances. But Jessica was tantalizing; a challenge and a worthy opponent, one who had eluded him, which, in itself, was quite remarkable. He was going to enjoy their game of cat and mouse.

Stefan picked up Jessica's cell phone and dialed Karl's number. "Karl, I believe I have someone here that you know," he began.

Upon completing their conversation, Stefan turned his attention to his captive.

"Now, my lovely Jessica, it's your turn," Stefan told her through the glass then re-entered the interrogation room. "I'm afraid to say, my dear, that you won't be with us much longer," Stefan told Jessica as he walked around her one last time."It's been a pleasure..." was all Jessica heard before Stefan covered her mouth and nose with the chloroform-soaked rag. She struggled until the drug overpowered her and she went limp.

"Now, are you ready?" Stefan asked the white-uniformed guard who appeared from the shadows.

The man nodded, and Stefan held her hair out of the way while the doctor made a small incision on the nape of her neck. Using tweezers, he inserted a tiny chip. The opening was sealed using superglue and was unnoticeable.

"That wasn't so bad, was it, my dear?" Stefan said, letting her hair fall back into place. "I bet you'll hardly even notice it."

He cut her duct tape bindings, picked up her limp body, and brought her back into his private room, which was more of a studio apartment, complete with living room, kitchenette, and bedroom.

"I think we have enough time," Stefan said as he excitedly began undressing her.

As much as he liked more life to his conquests, he didn't have time to fight her right now. It bothered him somewhat that lifeless bodies aroused him so much. Maybe from too many hours spent with the inflatable dolls of his youth.

With Jessica blissfully unaware, Stefan ravished her in the few minutes they had before it was time to leave. As unresponsive as she was, at least she was warm inside, something he much preferred to the women he had defiled just before rigor mortis set in.

"Ooh, honey, we have to go. Was it good for you?" Stefan whispered in her ear as he dressed her again.

Only one shoe. It would have to do. He carried her out to the custom Mercedes Limo, equipped with bulletproof glass, a full bar, and spacious seating. Stefan plopped her down on the seat across from him and lit up another Cuban cigar as they took off to meet Karl.

The drug faded, and Jessica slowly woke, her hands bound. She immediately succumbed to the nausea induced by the swaying of the car and the heavy cigar smoke, lurching forward, and vomiting all over Stefan's shoes.

"You whore!" Stefan, disgusted, slapped her once again, furious his imported alligator shoes now were soiled with the remains of Jessica's previous meal. His anger subsided as he studied her with fondness, remembering the afternoon in his quarters. He took his handkerchief and tried to wipe away a bit of residue on the corner of her mouth.

"Here," he poured her a shot of whiskey and held it to her mouth. "Something to wash the taste out of your mouth."

She sucked the fluid into her mouth. As much as Jessica hated hard liquor, at least the strong taste would mask the nasty vomit residue.

In returning to his seat across from her, he tried to sit at the same time the limo rounded a corner. He tried to compensate for the centrifugal force of the turn and almost righted himself when he lost his footing and slipped in the vomit on the floor, plopping solidly in the mess.

Stefan hissed to the driver, "Give me your jacket," which was thrown on the floor to cover the mess. Jessica, knowing full well that Stefan would explode at any moment, kept her smirk to herself but couldn't think of a more deserving end to their journey. Well, there were a few better options... and she would love to explore those possibilities herself if Karl didn't get to him first.

* * *

As soon as Karl and Mr. Hughes realized that Jessica had been abducted, they knew they needed to formulate a plan. They were expecting to be contacted by abductors wanting to exchange Jessica for the ledgers. Waiting for that call was excruciating.

Immediately, Mr. Hughes started making phone calls, gathering his troops from the local Jewish community center that the Museum of Tolerance supported. It provided a safe haven, a neutral territory, even for gang members, who used the facility's gym, swimming pool, and weight room. Scores of young men of every race met at the JCC, agreeing to leave not only their weapons, but their differences, and more importantly, their gang affiliations, at the door — or they were no longer welcome.

Mr. Hughes spent his free time volunteering at the center for the past twenty years and had befriended these young men, even admiring them for their desire to rise above their circumstances. He had seen some get out of the ghetto and be successful; others succumbed to the violence and left in caskets. In return for his unconditional acceptance regardless of their background, Mr. Hughes had earned their respect and undying allegiance.

The response was overwhelming. Once word was out, a small army volunteered to help. Mr. Hughes had no idea the impact he had made with the generations of boys, now men, that he had befriended.

Both Karl and Mr. Hughes had decided to drive vehicles to the destination. Once there, Mr. Hughes was greeted by scores of current and former members of opposing gangs, wishing to pay it forward for Mr. Hughes. As much as he tried to hide it, a single tear made its way down his cheek, betraying his emotions to these tough guys. He couldn't help it — it was amazing.

They went over their strategy, then over it again, and were ready to be in their positions as soon as the call came in. After hanging up, the boiling-mad, red-faced Karl announced, "Are you ready? We've got an hour."

"Right. I think we've got our backs covered," said a nervous Mr. Hughes as he glanced around the warehouse, the gang members giving him nods as he made eye contact with each of them. "Since we snuck out of my office, I'm sure they don't have a clue that you and I are together. I've cued the driver to leave and make their way over here with the other vehicle."

Everyone took their positions in the shadows, and Karl climbed into his rental SUV and parked it in the center of the vacant warehouse.

As expected, Stefan's front men soon arrived to check out the location. As professional as these guys were, they were up against street fighters adept at hiding from authorities.

* * *

"We're here," Stefan said into the phone. "It will soon be finished."

They had arrived at the deserted area. A second car carrying a few more of Stefan's subordinates arrived immediately after. Another vehicle pulled up, and the massive garage door opened to reveal a lone SUV parked in the center of the warehouse, the driver's door out of view. The other vehicle drove to the opposite side of the SUV, out of Stefan's sight, and parked.

Karl exited the SUV as the garage door lifted and, as the other vehicle drove near him, walked around the rental, giving the impression that he had just arrived. He had to use every ounce of self-control to not storm the limo and rescue Jessica. For the first time in his life, he wanted to kill someone.

Just before the driver opened the door for them, Stefan leaned over Jessica one last time.

"You were lovely," he said, brushing his lips on the top of her head. "But all good things must come to an end." He pinched the soft underside of her forearm, making Jessica wince. "I'll be watching you. One wrong move, and it'll all be over for you."

Stefan exited as the door was opened for him. The passengers of the second car piled out and stood menacingly behind him.

"Mr. Conrad, so nice to finally meet you in person." He greeted Karl from twenty feet away. "Now, where are my records?"

"Where's Jessica? Nothing happens until I see that she's safe," Karl growled.

"As you wish." Stefan gave the nod to his driver, and Jessica was pulled out of the limo. Stefan grabbed her arm. "Here you are. See, she's safe." He brushed his cheek against her hair, still looking at Karl for a reaction. Karl's veins popped out of his neck. "We had a very... nice... time together."

Karl gasped at the sight of her, bruised, swollen, disheveled. His anger rose to intolerable levels. The sight of her flamed Karl's underlying rage.

Jessica, repulsed, wrenched free of Stefan's grasp on her arm and ran to Karl, her hands still bound. Karl embraced her briefly, never taking his eyes off Stefan.

"Are you okay?" he whispered in her ear.

She nodded, wild eyed, knowing that the next few moments would be critical. "Follow my lead. We've got friends here," he whispered.

She nodded, and they reluctantly disengaged from one another, Karl moving her directly behind him.

"Well, it seems that she prefers you. Fine, take her. I'm finished with her anyway," Stefan said with contempt, adding under his breath, "You won't get far."

"I hope she's worth it. Now for your end of the deal. Where is it? An even exchange. I wouldn't expect anything less from a man of your character."

"Fair enough. Here you go," Karl replied as he tossed him the keys.

Stefan caught the keys with a snap of his wrist, never breaking the locked gaze with Karl. He tossed them to one of his henchmen.

"Open it," Stefan commanded.

Unlocking the doors by the keyless remote, the henchman opened the side door to reveal a load of old boxes. Laying on top of one of the sealed boxes was one of the ledgers. He picked it up and brought it to Stefan, who briefly glanced through it. "Looks authentic. Good. You were wise not to play any more games."

Giving a head motion to his men, they drew their weapons.

"Any last words, Mr. Conrad? Or should I say, Heydrich?"

"I'd put those away if I were you," Karl said, Jessica cowering behind him. "You didn't believe I wouldn't have some kind of insurance in place for us to get out of here alive, did you?"

Stefan held his hand up, halting his previous orders. He had thought it had been too easy, that Karl was too cooperative.

"I'm listening, but remember, the guns are still pointed directly at you, so don't try anything you will regret," Stefan said.

"That SUV and everything in it is set to explode if we're not safely out of here within fifteen minutes. My pyrotechnic friends have even hooked up something that will trigger the device if the weight distribution changes by ten pounds. Or was it five? Geez, I don't remember," Karl said with sarcasm, "but what that means is that if you want those stupid dusty old books, you *have* to let us walk out of here safely right now."

The silence was deafening. Stefan's henchmen looked at each other nervously, taking a step back, away from the vehicle and toward the door.

Finally, Stefan spoke in a level, terse tone. "Go then. You've served your purpose. But know this — if the detonation is not cancelled immediately after you leave, we will have no problems tracking you down. We have known your every move from the beginning. And then your deaths would not be as quick as they would have been here. You will watch as I slowly torture the woman until she dies before your eyes. Then we will take twice as long to let you die."

As much as he didn't want to let them go, the tracking chip they had placed in Jessica's neck assured they could find them at any moment.

Karl quickly escorted Jessica by the elbow out the door. They were almost out of harm's way when Stefan offered his last barb.

"I hope she satisfies you more than she did me," Stefan sneered. "I particularly liked that mole on her thigh."

Karl came to a dead halt, silhouetted in the door, inches from freedom. The words struck Jessica to the core, her blood running cold with the fear of the unknown atrocities Stefan had performed. Karl's last shred of self-control flew out the window, making it impossible for him to maintain the fragile hold he had over his emotions.

"Run," he told Jessica and pushed her forward as he spun on his heel and charged like a bull toward his nemesis.

"Oh, boy, here it comes..." Mr. Hughes said under his breath from his hiding place. "*Now!*" he screamed into the walkie-talkie.

Karl seemed to move in slow motion as he stormed toward Stefan, bent on making him pay for everything he had done to Jessica. Just as the surprised henchmen raised their weapons, they were descended on by all the gang members, who appeared out of every shadow and came streaming through the doorway.

Mr. Hughes intercepted Jessica, and they were whisked away into the waiting getaway car. He was distraught that Karl had chosen to fight, but he wanted to get Jessica to safety, far away from the mayhem.

"Drive," he ordered.

"No!" Jessica tried to open the door, Mr. Hughes quickly restraining her. "We can't leave Karl."

"I'm sorry, but we have to get you out of here. He has friends covering his back." He said a quick prayer. "Karl will be joining us soon."

Their car sped away.

The gang members overpowered the neo-Nazis. Stefan was unprotected and unprepared for the full brunt of an unabashed, thundering Karl as he barreled into him, knocking them both to the floor. They rolled in a struggle, the larger, adrenaline-pumped Karl having the upper hand, seeming invincible. The gang members had quickly taken care of the others and were enjoying the sight of Karl pommeling Stefan, eventually pulling Karl away before it was too late. The director had told them they needed Stefan.

Karl was still seeing red and exhibiting almost superhuman strength. It took several of the brawniest gang members to pry him off Stefan. Although Stefan now lay there, a bloody mess, he looked up at Karl with his wobbly head and smiled, a tooth missing.

"Ah, I found your Achilles heel," Stefan said as he spat blood.

Karl wrenched himself away and knocked Stefan out. His disgust for this vile man replaced his rage. Karl gave him one last kick for good measure and ran out the door.

"Jessica?" he shouted, frantically looking up and down the street for her.

"Hey, man, she's okay. Mr. H got her out of here," he was told. "Here, get in. My ride can take you there."

Karl got in the souped-up street racer and was driven a few blocks away to where Mr. Hughes waited.

"She's in here," Mr. Hughes said, opening the car door. Karl could only see Jessica's frightened eyes in the shadows. She was cocooned in a blanket Mr. Hughes had found in the trunk, attempting to help her shivering.

"The ledgers..." Jessica said through her chattering teeth, craning to look behind her toward the warehouse.

"It's okay. Our guys are taking care of it," Karl reassured her, but Jessica's incredulous look made him continue, "Seriously. Right, Ryan?"

The driver turned around and flashed a huge grin, the light catching the diamond stud embedded in his tooth. "Absolutely."

Just then, the rented SUV careened around the corner and fell into line behind their vehicle, peeling off in another direction after a few blocks.

Jessica snuggled deep into the crook of Karl's arm.

"You okay?" he whispered, kissing the top of her head.

She nodded silently, staring blankly ahead, a tear finding its way down her cheek.

They drove about an hour, making their way from the city to a sprawling residential area. Estate houses lined the treed, manicured streets. The car slowed at one of the homes, and the huge wrought iron gates swung open. At the end of the winding drive, light bathed a palatial ivory-colored mansion.

"Here we are," Ryan announced.

Both Karl and Jessica had dozed off during the drive, adrenaline replaced by mental and physical exhaustion.

Jessica finally had some solid rest, safe in Karl's arms with no visions to haunt her. Karl was the one who had been dreaming this time. No nightmares; just Jessica and him alone on a beach. How he hated to return to the real world — he knew he'd pick it up another time.

The car door opened, and they were escorted up the stairs to the front entrance. The ten-foot double doors opened to reveal a magnificent entry; cream colored marble floors mirrored a sweeping grand stairway that showcased the crystal chandelier.

"Welcome. Thank God you are safe. Come in, come in. Make yourself at home." The tiny white-haired lady barely stood five feet tall. "Hello, I'm Pearl Steinman, but you can call me Miss Pearl."

Their petite hostess' regal and gracious demeanor indicated she was the matriarch of this estate. Getting her first good look at Karl and Jessica, she immediately took stock of what they needed and made provisions for them.

"Heavens to Betsy! What in the world happened to you two? No, never mind, maybe I don't want to know... Lord knows I've seen worse..." her voice trailed off then re-energized. "Now, now, you must come with me, and I'll get you squared away."

She hooked arms with Jessica and Karl and escorted them toward the stairway. "Follow me."

Miss Pearl grandly sat in the chairlift at the bottom of the stairway, pushed a button, and glided up the stairs.

Karl and Jessica stood at the bottom of the stairs, engrossed.

"What's keeping you? Come on."

Not quite sure whether or not she was in some kind of disjointed dream, Jessica began her ascent up the stairs.

"We're coming," Karl said as he followed Jessica up the steps. In her exhausted state, the walk up the stairs nearly caused Jessica to collapse. Their hostess, Pearl, was waiting for them at the top.

"I want what you have," Jessica told her, nodding toward the stair glider.

"Honey, it's all yours," Miss Pearl replied with a chuckle. "Don't know what I'd do without it. I did install an elevator — it's at the end of the hall — but it's not nearly as fun."

She led Jessica and Karl to adjoining rooms. She took Jessica to hers first and entered Karl's through a connecting door.

"Here you are. There are fresh clothes in the closet. Help yourself to whatever you like that fits you. Out on the balcony is a hot tub. Jessica, a good soak will do you wonders."

"Thank you so much," Jessica said, giving Pearl a hug.

"It's my pleasure. I will be sending up some food for you. Your job right now is just to relax. You're safe now."

"Thank you, Miss Pearl, you are very gracious," Karl said as he walked her into the hall. Once out of Jessica's earshot, he continued, "She's had a really hard day. I don't know what all they did to her. If you have something that would help her sleep better, please send that up, too."

"Of course. You just take care of her." Miss Pearl gave Karl a hug, then pulled away and looked him square in the eye, leaning way back since he was so tall. "You two are very cute together," she said with a wink. "May God richly bless you."

Jessica didn't waste any time shedding her filthy clothes and blanket that had been wrapped around her. *Burning would be too good for them*, she thought as she threw them in a pile. The lingering cigar odor reminded her of her captors, something she wanted to purge from her memory.

Naked, she stepped gingerly into the warm water. The soothing fragrance of aromatherapy candles gently combined with the sweetness of the evening air. She immersed herself, then raised her head out of the water like a sea nymph, her hair beautifully plastered to her head.

"Ah…" Jessica sighed as she felt her body finally begin to release its tension. She rested her head on the cushy pillow made specifically for tub use and let herself soak in the decadent pleasure of doing nothing.

After some time, Jessica began the arduous task of removing the blood, sweat, and dirt from her pores using a large sea sponge and body wash from a basket along the tub.

"Need someone to wash your back?"

Jessica jumped.

"I brought dinner. I know you're exhausted, so I thought I'd bring it to you while it was still hot," Karl said as he carried a tray with several covered plates onto the balcony and set it on the edge of the hot tub. He lifted the cover off the main dish.

"Mm... Steak."

Jessica's stomach growled audibly as she realized she was famished.

"Well, someone's hungry," Karl said, cutting up the meat for her. "Medium rare. Pink in the middle. Perfect. Well, I hope that's how you like it," Karl said.

"Perfect. Times like these make me thankful I'm not a vegetarian. Give me meat," Jessica said as Karl delivered a forkful to her mouth. Never had she tasted anything as delicious. "I've died and gone to heaven.'

Next, he fed her asparagus, then sauteed mushrooms, then mashed potatoes and gravy.

Aside from her taste buds crying for joy at the explosion of flavor after not eating since breakfast, what made this meal even more delicious was that it was being hand fed to her by the most remarkable man she had ever met.

Karl served himself a forkful in between serving Jessica, while she chewed.

Miss Pearl had sent up a wonderful merlot with the meal. "You must, of course, have a red wine with your red meat," she had insisted.

The combination of the hot bath easing her sore muscles and her full tummy, washed down with several glasses of the fine merlot, worked its magic. Jessica was completely relaxed.

Karl took the empty tray into the other room.

Jessica rested her head on the bath pillow and closed her eyes. *What a nice ending to such a horrific day*, she thought.

She heard a small splash. Her eyes flew open. Karl had joined her. The tub had plenty of room for both.

"Ah, this is nice," Karl said, resting his head on the opposite edge, his legs intertwining with hers.

"Mm, I like pretzeling with you," Jessica said.

"Pretzeling? What's that?" Karl inquired.

"This, what we're doing — twisting our legs together like we're pretzels," Jessica explained, demonstrating.

"Ah, yes. Love the pretzel," Karl replied. "But my favorite is the sugar," he said as he scooted over to her side of the tub and slowly kissed her lips, sweet with wine. "It's good to mix sweet with salty, you know," Karl said between kisses.

Jessica had thought she was too exhausted to do one more thing but surprised herself at the intensity of her response to Karl's attention. With renewed energy, she forgot every bad thing of the day. Nothing else existed at this moment but Karl, Jessica, and the starry sky. Their eyes locked as they twisted together, waves lapping the hot tub's edges, becoming stormier until white caps and waves splashed onto the balcony.

* * *

The view of the balcony was perfect. The two men hidden in the tree at the perimeter of the estate were enjoying the show. Most of the time, surveillance was boring; sitting for hours, babysitting a whole bunch of nothing. But today was different. This made up for all the other insignificant hours wasted. The show ended when the pair went inside and turned off the lights.

"Well, it was good while it lasted," one told the other, and they settled in for the night.

* * *

"This morning, we'll be meeting with Stanley Guhl," Mr. Hughes announced while buttering his toast. "He is an expert in Nazi paraphernalia. We need to have an outside source authenticate the records. It is crucial. If these ledgers do not have unquestionable verification that they are the real deal, the items will never be returned to their rightful owners. It would be sad if these books are forgeries, created for someone's personal gain, and not honored."

"Um, I see," Karl said between bites of his eggs Benedict. "I didn't think of that."

"More coffee?" Miss Pearl asked her guests as she strained to lift the porcelain carafe, her shaky hands causing the pot to wobble crazily.

"I've got it." Karl rescued the pot from her frail grasp. Miss Pearl cast him a grateful glance.

"Yes, please," Jessica replied to the offer, holding the dainty hand-painted cup toward Karl. "Just half a cup please. Lots of cream. I like it weak."

"Why, that's not coffee at all," Mr. Hughes commented. "It's just hot brown milk. Real coffee drinkers like me like their coffee strong enough to chew."

"Is the expert coming here?" Jessica asked, hopefully. She was enjoying being pampered and didn't want it to end.

"No, I'm sorry, the mountain must go to Mohammed," Mr. Hughes told her. "You'll find him interesting. We will be meeting with him in a rather unusual place."

Karl and Jessica exchanged curious expressions.

"This man is a meticulous researcher. He's published many papers on the Third Reich and is one of the world's top resources in this area. His word is the final word. His stamp of approval is all we need," Mr. Hughes explained. "He does this in his spare time — it's his passion — but we're meeting him at his place of work; a family business that he's inherited. I'll just leave it at that."

*　*　*

They had driven about an hour when the caravan slowed and turned into the drive of the Peaceful Haven mortuary.

"You've got to be kidding," Karl muttered.

They saw a fleet of hearses lined up in perfect rows, their long black bodies highly waxed, not a speck of dust to be found anywhere.

The first vehicle carried Mr. Hughes, Jessica, and Karl; the second being the rental SUV full of precious cargo with Ryan at the wheel. They drove around to the back of the complex where they stopped at a garage door with an intercom.

"We're here," Mr. Hughes said into the intercom.

The garage door slowly opened, and they drove down into the darkness, descending into a lower-level parking garage under the extensive mortuary. As the door shut behind them, the lights came on full blast. This was where the hearses were loaded with the remains of the deceased in caskets to take their final trip to the cemetery. Stanley Guhl ran a streamlined business, allowing the bereaved to focus on their grief.

Ryan was left to guard the vehicles as the rest of the group walked toward the elevators. Jessica felt an overwhelming heaviness descend upon her. The elevator was long enough to transport a casket. She then understood why she felt so sad; so many souls had been transported through this lift. She clung to Karl's arm a little too tightly.

The Girl from Ipanema playing over the sound system was the only sound as they ascended.

Although his customer's sorrow was inevitable, Stanley Guhl's intent for this funeral home was to emphasize the positive, which was a daunting task. He'd experienced all varieties of services for those who passed. The long, drawn-out expected death by cancer or old age, where death was prepared for; the suicides, where a huge disparity of emotions was present. The innocent victims of violent crimes were the loudest mourners, and the most emotional were the families who lost their children or babies.

But for everyone who grieved, there were also the few heartless bastards that he had no stomach for. Their attitude was that death was inevitable and, in most cases, it was someone they cared little about, or a family member who had been a burden, or the passing had been the only stumbling block to inheritance.

Stanley's favorite type of service was when the deceased had a clear idea of eternity, and those gathering to mourn had been asked to celebrate instead. There were tears for the loss of the loved one because they would be missed, but laughing as stories were reminisced and love exuded from all.

Stanley Guhl grew up in this environment. His father had been a mortician, as had his father before him. His grandfather had immigrated to America just before Hitler took power. He didn't like what was happening but primarily left because Germany was suffering from a depression, and he wanted to start fresh in the Land of Opportunity.

Stanley had never liked all the black, somber, creepy decor of the funeral home as a child, and after spending any time at all helping his father at the business, he always welcomed the bright and cheerful, colorful personal residence. When it came time for college, Stanley went to Princeton, majoring in history and business; one for his passion, one for money. By the time his father retired, Stanley was expected to continue in his shoes.

As soon as he took over, gone was the dreary décor, replaced with calming designer colors. Flowers were an important part of his business, and they added to the cheerful rooms to counteract the sadness. He felt there was already too much grief, so why not do his part to cheer people up a bit? He had conducted his own personal study to see if his changes made a difference and found the tears and anger were less and the strain not as much a burden. The bonus was that even the bereaved families making funerary arrangements weren't as short tempered.

He always knew it was expected of him to take over the family business, but he was also determined to fulfill his own desires and walk his own path. So, Stanley had established a well-oiled machine of a team at the Peaceful Haven who did their jobs so well that he wasn't really needed, which allowed him to travel, pursuing his love for history.

The papers he had written were published in all the major periodicals, and he was becoming well known for his penchant for detail and accuracy. His claim to fame had been when he debunked a previously authenticated letter from Hitler himself, proving the paper wasn't even manufactured until the 1950s. Since then, Stanley had proven his expertise so many times that the very mention of his name endorsing a project carried authenticity beyond reproach.

He had claimed an area of the building for his research. On the second floor, Stanley had a small laboratory. That is where they found him.

"Hello, I'm Stanley Guhl." He introduced himself, jumping up from his chair as the group entered. He looked them all over and lingered on the bumps and bruises still on Jessica's face. "What happened to you?" he asked.

"Oh, nothing really," she lied.

"Ghoul. Kind of an odd name to hear in a funeral home." Karl chuckled.

"It's Guhl. G-U-H-L. German," Stanley said with the patience of someone who had heard it before. "Hey, we had to find *some* kind of business that fit the name, didn't we?" he quipped, breaking the ice. He motioned for them to take a seat in an area with several couches.

"Stanley, it's good to see you again. Keeping busy?" Mr. Hughes asked as they settled in. "Indeed. Always working late," Stanley replied. "What brings you here? This is highly unusual for you to honor me with your presence."

"This," Jessica said and pulled one of the ledgers out of her briefcase.

Before taking it from her, Stanley went over to his lab table and donned white linen gloves. "I don't want to contaminate it with the oils on my fingers."

Jessica handed the book to him sheepishly, then wiped her fingers on her pants. "Hm..." Stanley began his examination. "Interesting... A new find, I take it, since I have no recollection of this volume existing."

He had moved over to his microscope, looking closely at the paper, the ink, the binding method, the handwriting. He rolled his chair over to his computer, pulling up files from his database, consumed in his study of the manuscript.

"Coffee?" Stanley's assistant had arrived with a huge tray of cups, a coffee pot, and pastries.

"Yes," Karl and Jessica responded simultaneously.

"Please," Mr. Hughes chimed in, then in an aside to Karl and Jessica, he said, "I did not give Mr. Guhl any information about what we were bringing him. I wanted his assessment to be completely unbiased and independent with no outside influence."

"Wouldn't it have helped him?" Jessica asked.

"Ha! He doesn't need any help. Plus, it could have hurt us instead by tainting his own judgment by having our information," Mr. Hughes replied. "We want him to draw his own conclusions, so his report has no way to be refuted."

Eventually, Stanley Guhl concluded his testing and swung his chair around to face them. "Well, I don't know where you got this, but I can say with full authority that this is a record-keeping ledger that was compiled by several different individuals, SS personnel, during the beginning of World War II. The ink, the paper, the ledger itself, plus the actual handwriting on many pages I recognized to be specific SS officers. You've got the real deal here. I'm sure this will bring a high dollar on the auction block. I may even be a bidder. There are tons of Nazi memorabilia collectors who would jump at the chance to obtain a previously unknown manuscript of this caliber."

"We have more. Would you like to see?" Karl asked.

"More? How many more?" Stanley's voice trembled with excitement.

"Let's just show him. They're in the car," Mr. Hughes said.

The group headed for the elevator. Stanley punched the down button repeatedly until the doors opened. "C'mon, tell me. How many more?" Stanley asked, shuffling from one leg to the other. "More than two?"

"Yes," Karl answered, kind of liking this game.

"More than… ten?"

"Yes."

The suspense was killing him. As the elevator door opened at the garage level, Stanley bolted out the door, recognizing the two unfamiliar vehicles.

The *beep-beep* of the doors being unlocked alerted Ryan they had arrived. He started to intercept Stanley, initially mistaking him for the enemy, but was motioned to hold off as Stanley swung the doors wide open.

"Holy shit," Stanley said as he pulled the linen gloves from his pants pocket and began rifling through the boxes. He could barely catch his breath. "Do you have any idea what you've got here? Am I dreaming?" Stanley said as he turned to Mr. Hughes. "Pinch me. Seriously, hit me hard. I want to make sure I'm awake."

Mr. Hughes had known Stanley Guhl for a long time and had wanted many times to punch him. He hauled off a good clip to Stanley's shoulder.

"Ow!" Stanley yelled, reeling from the pain. "Awesome. It is real. Who *are* you people?"

"We'll need you to verify every book. It's very important, but we don't have much time."

Stanley stopped cold in the middle of perusing one of the boxes and straightened. "What's going on here?"

"Listen, Stanley, I don't want to put you in danger, but someone doesn't want us to have this information. I have a good idea why. We took precautions so they don't know where we are. I had to have your seal of authenticity before moving forward," Mr. Hughes explained.

"So, is someone trying to kill you? Is it *that* kind of danger?" Stanley asked.

"Well, I'd have to say... yes," Mr. Hughes replied.

Stanley didn't react like anyone expected. "Cool."

"What?" Karl didn't understand this guy at all.

Stanley backtracked. "Well, okay, not *cool* that someone is trying to kill you, and rest assured it has nothing to do with my line of business or anything, but it's cool that I'm involved in something a *lot* more exciting than cremating bodies."

"So, you're okay with helping us?" Jessica asked.

"By all means. I'm offering my services and my facility in any capacity that you need," Stanley said, giving her a wink. "Let's get these upstairs."

In a small room on the garage level, Stanley found two collapsible gurneys normally used to transport coffins from the mortuary to the basement for loading the hearse. Ryan and Karl helped Stanley load the boxes onto one gurney, then filled another with the remaining boxes. They transported the loads up to his lab via elevator; Stanley and Mr. Hughes with the first load, Karl and Jessica with the second.

Once alone in the lift, Karl asked Jessica, "How do you feel?"

"Doing okay," Jessica said, idly scratching the back of her head. She still couldn't shake the heaviness that poured over her, attributing it to her location. She felt unable to voice her uneasiness to Karl yet, still aching from the bruises and soreness from yesterday's events. Yesterday... Was it only a day ago?

The door opened, and they escorted the boxes to the lab. Stanley had brought up the first load and was already hard at work, moving surprisingly fast. They formed a quirky assembly line — all were wearing white gloves, Karl passing the books to Stanley; Stanley reviewing each prior to passing them to Mr. Hughes, who was photographing each page prior to passing them to Jessica to store in museum-quality storage bins.

"The acid in the cardboard boxes eats away at biodegradable objects over time. We don't want any damage to these records, so we'll store them properly," Stanley had instructed.

Each book was individually sealed in its own plastic bag, the kind used to preserve delicate documents, then carefully packed in crates.

"Wow. You sure don't waste any time, do you?" Karl observed.

Stanley didn't look up as he replied, "Well, I have already gone through most of the work on the first ledger, so now I'm merely noting that each bears the same similarities. The first one always takes the longest," he said, methodically reviewing each book.

"I was aware that these records were kept during World War II and, like everyone else, thought these were destroyed at the end of the regime, either by Hitler's staff or by the Allies when they came through. I'm still trying to get my head around the fact that I'm holding them in my hands."

Stanley took a moment to admire the ledgers.

"Now, these photo albums are remarkable. They were compiled from confiscated art and intended to be presented to Hitler, who was not only a lover of art, but fancied himself to be an artist, although not a very good one. It's unclear whether or not Hitler actually saw these art albums, but we know that forty-one of the one hundred are accounted for. You have fifty here, so these few boxes of photo albums comprise the largest collection that any one person has ever had... So, that totals ninety-one albums that we know are in existence. Either there really wasn't exactly one hundred albums to begin with, or there's a few more floating around somewhere... A souvenir, perhaps, of a Nazi or Allied soldier."

The group methodically worked in silence as they absorbed what Stanley had told them. After carting their treasure across the country, it was gratifying to hear some of the actual history. Wearing the protective gloves, Jessica flipped through the pages of one of the art albums. When Stanley finished reviewing a book, he handed it to her, and she thumbed through each. After perusing several, a certain painting caught her eye.

"I've seen this before," she said. "Karl, this was in your grandfather's home."

The eerie feeling she'd felt when the painting cried out to her returned, the image of the woman's mouth moving forever burned in her memory. She shuddered.

"Let me see," Karl and Stanley said simultaneously.

They sandwiched Jessica as they crowded in to look.

"Yes, that's right, Jessica. That's hung over the fireplace ever since I can remember," Karl exclaimed.

Stanley pointed below the photo. "You see there, it says, *Portrait by Vermeer*? I'd have to contest that, because I've never seen this one, but it's a possibility. You know some of the art was purchased from wealthy Jews, one of those deals where they didn't actually *want* to sell but were told they'd get some kind of amnesty if they sold them for Hitler's collection. He was starting an art museum in Nuremberg. Now some of the descendants believe they have a right to those paintings, but there are sales receipts that the paintings were legally purchased, even though under those circumstances. Where is the painting now?"

Karl opened his mouth to answer but was interrupted by Stanley.

"Wait, don't tell me. I don't want to know. Just tell me that it's safe."

"It is," Karl assured him. "Well, maybe I need to look through these, too, and see if I recognize anything else."

"There was wonderful art everywhere in Karl's grandpa's home," Jessica told Stanley and Mr. Hughes. "Absolutely incredible."

"I'm almost finished reviewing all the books, and then I'll draw up a letter of authenticity," Stanley told the group, going back to perusing the volumes.

* * *

"Where are they now?" the grizzled old man barked. "What is taking you so long?" Hans Sprechter was frustrated beyond measure.

"We know exactly where they are and are watching them. Right now, they are at a mortuary — the..." He glanced at the slip of paper in his hand. "The Peaceful Haven Funeral Home. We ran a check on it, and the owner is Stanley Guhl, a WWII memorabilia expert on the side."

"Hm... a mortuary, is it? How fitting. Well, guaranteed they are not making funeral arrangements, but maybe they should," the old man said with a wry smile. "We've waited long enough. Make your move *now*."

The aged SS icon spat out his words and almost choked in a small seizure. The recipient of the old man's anger nodded and left the room. Although the old geezer didn't have much time left on this Earth, his younger cohort still had to play the role of his puppet.

"Go," he said into the receiver.

* * *

The men stationed around the mortuary descended upon it nonchalantly, blending in with mourners arriving to pay their last respects to a loved one. The only way to distinguish them was their telltale earpiece.

Two of the men made their way to the office and asked to speak to Stanley Guhl.

"Mr. Guhl, there is someone here to see you," the voice crackled over the intercom in the laboratory. "They are here in your office. Said something about making special arrangements for a burial. He insisted on talking only to you."

Stanley rolled his eyes as he spoke to his comrades. "Wouldn't you know? All day I sat in my office doing nothing, and now that I'm busy, they come out of the woodwork." Then, pressing the on button of the intercom, he said, "Uh, I'm in the middle of something right now. See if they can return later."

Stanley clicked on the security monitor for the office and saw two men in dark suits nervously awaiting him.

"No, go on," Mr. Hughes interjected. "We're on the last ledgers and have taken up too much of your time already..." His words trailed off as he noticed Jessica.

She was glued to the monitor, studying the men as she walked closer to the screen to get a better look. An twitch coursed over her face.

"There's something familiar about this man," she whispered, touching the screen. "Is it possible to zoom in on his right hand?" She had seen that symbol on the ring before.

"The Holy Roman Empire," Stanley and Jessica said at the same time.

"We've been made," Stanley said.

The other three turned and looked at him.

"What?" he said, shrugging and extending his hands. "That's what they always say when your cover's blown. They say it all the time on TV."

"Well, you're right. We've gotta get out of here *fast*," Karl said as they closed the last crate and gathered their belongings.

"I'll go meet with them, just like they want, and delay them for a few minutes so you can be gone before they know it," Stanley offered.

"No," Jessica insisted. She knew they wouldn't hesitate to dispose of him.

"Yes, I must go. I need to buy you some time. I know every way out of this place. I'm calling 9-1-1 now, and the cops will be here in five minutes. Take the elevator down to the garage. I'll make sure you and your cargo get out of here safely," Stanley replied determinedly.

"He's right," Karl said reluctantly. "Let's not waste time. Hurry up."

The trio hurried the crates onto the funerary gurneys and entered the elevator, pinning themselves against the wall. This time, it only took one trip since the ledgers were now in a more compact form.

"Let's go!"

The garage door of the Peaceful Haven Funeral Home opened and out flew the SUV with Ryan at the wheel closely followed by Mr. Hughes' car. They tore out of the parking lot, almost clipping a mourner or two for the memorial of Mortimer Jones, whose name was on the morgue's marquee. As soon as they had peeled out and rounded the corner, two dark sedans fell in line after them.

Once they disappeared, out of the garage came the hearse carrying the deceased. Several vehicles fell in line behind the hearse just before complete confusion descended as one hearse, then another and another, emerged from the garage, each heading in a different direction. The poor mourners for Mortimer Jones didn't know which way to turn, unsure which hearse they needed to follow.

Stanley Guhl entered his office to face the two gentlemen. On impulse, he clicked his heels and greeted them.

"Heil," he said, raising his arm in a Hitler salute. One of the two caught himself just after he began to automatically respond, while the other just shook his head at his partner.

"Idiot," he muttered, still shaking his head. At least formalities were not necessary.

"Where are they?" the ringed man demanded. "Or do you need prompting?"

He deftly grabbed Stanley's secretary and swiftly brought a knife to her throat. He inhaled the scent of her neck as his hot breath touched her skin.

"Mm, I like that perfume. Is that Beautiful?"

The frightened secretary nodded.

"Don't hurt her! I have the information you are looking for. Let her go, and I'll take you to where they've hidden the ledgers," Stanley said.

"Uh, no, don't think so... I believe Miss, uh..." He glanced at the nameplate at her desk. "Miss Davenport should accompany us, just in case."

The captor cocked his head as he received some information through his earpiece.

Stanley only had a few moments to devise his plan. "I'm sure you've just heard that your prey has flown the coop," Stanley began.

The large man rolled his eyes. This guy was straight out of a B movie. Then he drew the knife across Miss Davenport's neck in a mock cutting action.

"Okay, okay." Stanley turned serious. "They escaped but didn't have time to take the goods. Just don't hurt Marti," Stanley said, falling back into his corny lingo. "They brought them to me to authenticate awesome records. Did you see them?"

The hungry look in their eyes confirmed they had not.

Stanley had to think fast. "But, hey, they're just books, really. And not nearly as valuable as the life of my secretary."

"Or yours," he said.

"Uh, right... or mine." The sweat was beading on Stanley's forehead. "Hey, you know what? You can have them. They're very interesting, but not worth putting your life on the line for, if you know what I mean... but I'm not going to take you to them unless you guarantee you'll let both of us go."

"You're not exactly in a position to negotiate," he said, tightening his grip on Miss Davenport, making her squeal and her wide eyes wildly plead with Stanley.

"Well, you're the man with the weapon," Stanley conceded. "Right this way, gentlemen."

He led them to the elevator, where Stanley and the knifeless, not-so-bright thug, Bruno, reached for the down button at the same time. After a sharp look from Bruno, Stanley let him push the button.

They entered and descended without speaking as *The Girl from Ipanema* filtered through the music system. Bruno started humming along with the tune. His comrade shot him an incredulous glance to silenced him.

The elevator indicated the garage level, and the doors opened to meet an army of policemen, their weapons cocked and ready to shoot. Stanley, expecting this, took advantage of the men's surprise, knocked the knife away from Miss Davenport, and shoved the two out the elevator door. Seeing no viable alternative, they raised their hands in surrender, the music from the elevator filling the garage.

"Thanks, fellas," Stanley said, never in his life more relieved. "Book 'em, Dan-O."

9

WASHINGTON, DC - HOLOCAUST MUSEUM

"We received a call from the National Archives office. It seems some information has surfaced that may finally flush these guys out of hiding," the director, Mrs. Abernathy, told a colleague. "They beat our friend up pretty bad, but it made him realize the importance of the books they left behind. So, he had them checked out and, believe it or not, they're the real deal — written by the SS themselves."

She leaned closer to tell her more. "And *then*, we get a call from Mr. Hughes over at the Simon Wiesenthal Center, who told us to expect a guest. Guess what they're bringing? More of the same ledgers. Turns out it was the same two people who brought the first ones to the National Archives."

"Evidently, they've gotten someone's feather's ruffled, aye?" her coworker, Mrs. Porubcan noted.

Both went quiet, letting it sink in, then a light of realization turned on.

"*Shit!* They're coming here. Call security. They'll need protection. Hell, *we* probably need protection…" The words trailed from her mouth.

The ladies transformed into a machine of smooth efficiency.

Trained to handle extreme situations, they'd had their share of bomb threats and, with their military training years ago, knew how to handle just about any scenario. Two somewhat frumpy, middle-aged women that you'd more likely mistake for loving grandmas than threats, Mrs. Abernathy and Mrs. Porubcan were an unlikely force to be reckoned with.

* * *

"They're headed back into the city," the woman with the unibrow behind the computer relayed.

A blinking red blip moved slowly across the monitor in front of her.

* * *

"I can't help but wonder, how did they find us again?" Karl mused.

Jessica and Karl were squished together in the front seat with Pete, the driver of the hearse they had loaded the bins into.

"They must have put some kind of tracking thingee on the SUV. They had the chance when they checked it out in the warehouse," Karl said, trying to find the most logical explanation.

"Yeah, probably... Makes sense, but if they planned to take the vehicle, why do that?" Jessica replied, itching the back of her neck. "One thing's for sure. We've lost them for good now. There's no way they'd know where we are now. After all those hearses, they'd never have known which one to follow."

Still, it bothered Pete that one apparently determined "mourner" was still following them. They were getting closer to their destination, but he could see that the car was still dogging them, a few cars behind.

Jessica felt a little tickle at the back of her neck. She reached up to scratch it at the same time the driver's cell phone rang.

"Yes, we're about to arrive. We're not alone."

Upon hearing this, both Jessica and Karl looked behind them to see the dark sedan. "How could they have possibly known which hearse to follow?" Karl was perplexed. "There's no way."

Jessica's neck tickled again just prior to the cell phone ringing a second time.

"Yes, will do," Pete said and made a quick right turn, the centrifugal force plastering Jessica and Karl against the door.

"Karl, look at my neck," Jessica said, lifting her hair.

"Love to," Karl said, raising his eyebrows. "Any time."

"I'm serious. Is there anything back there? A spider?" Jessica said, shuddering.

Karl lifted Jessica's hair out of the way and examined the nape of her neck, involuntarily taking in her scent with a deep breath.

"No spider. There's a red scratch and a bump. That's all."

"That's weird. It tickled both times the phone just rang," Jessica said. Pete dialed his cell phone. Jessica's neck tickled again. "Do it again," Jessica said, panic in her voice.

Pete repeated his actions and her neck tickled again.

"Okay, why would a cell call make my neck itch?" Jessica asked.

"Do you have a knife?" Karl asked Pete.

"What?" Jessica said, covering the area with her hand.

"Hey, it's the only way to find out," Karl whispered. "I'll be gentle."

His hand covered hers, and as Jessica's relaxed, he was able to slide it down off her neck.

"Would this work?" Pete flipped open a large switchblade, the edge glinting in the sun.

Jessica screamed, "No!"

"Perfect." Karl took the knife, admiring it. "Nice. Make sure you drive nice and smooth."

"Roger, boss," said Pete, keeping an eye on the vehicle behind them.

"Karl, you can't really plan to cut into me with that... that... machete. Honestly, it's not bothering me anymore. It was merely a coincidence," pleaded Jessica.

"Well, I no longer believe in coincidences," Karl replied. "Now, hold still."

"Wait," Jessica cried, pulling a small bottle of sanitizer from her purse. "At least use this."

Karl laughed. Their driver also handed Karl a personal, foil-wrapped antiseptic wipe.

"What's this? I'm surrounded by germaphobes." Karl chuckled.

Pete defended himself. "Hey, there's a lot of germs at funerals."

"Yeah, well, with what we've been through, it's a good thing I have it," Jessica declared. "You're not cutting into me with that butcher knife without some precautions. Who knows *where* that has been," she glanced at Pete. "No offense."

"None taken," Pete replied with a slight grin.

Karl took both items, dabbed some antibacterial gel on her neck from the bottle, and used the towelette to wipe the blade.

"Now, hold still," Karl told her. "Here, hold on to my knee. Squeeze it if it hurts too much, and make sure to focus on relaxing your body. It won't hurt as much."

Jessica took a deep breath and grabbed Karl's leg with all her strength.

"Ow! Okay, not quite so tight. I need to concentrate here." Karl grimaced from Jessica's nails digging into his leg.

They stopped at a red light. Karl made a quick cut under the tiny bump and saw the edge of a nonorganic object. He carefully pushed the device out from under Jessica's skin through the small slit. It was a tiny rectangular microchip.

"Pete, do you have any Kleenex or napkins or anything to catch the blood?" Karl asked.

"Blood?" Jessica's grip tightened on Karl's knee.

"Ow! Stop that." Karl winced.

"How about this? It's clean." Pete handed him a cloth handkerchief.

"Wow, who uses these anymore? I think my grandpa had one," said Karl.

"My mom was big into recycling. Never liked the idea of throwaway snot wipers," Pete explained.

"Hey, remember me, the one bleeding to death?" Jessica interrupted.

Karl took the handkerchief from Pete, rolling his eyes at the embroidered monogram in the corner, and blotted Jessica's neck with it.

"What do you make of this?" Karl used the handkerchief to wipe Jessica's blood off the tiny chip. "Call me crazy, but I'm thinking this is how we've been followed."

Karl rolled down the window and threw it into a passing pickup truck's bed. "See ya," he said with a little wave.

The next stoplight they approached had just turned yellow. Pete slowed down as if about to stop and, just as the light turned red, floored it, running the red and almost getting hit by the cross traffic. It was enough to put a little distance between the hearse and its pursuer, just enough time for them to take the next two right turns and pull into an alleyway.

"There. Let's see if they find us now," Pete muttered.

* * *

"We've lost visual," the man in the car pursuing their prey told his superior over the phone.

They could still see the blinking icon on their monitor, which indicated that they were only a few blocks ahead.

"Noted. Proceed as planned. Use the tracking device, and let us know when they are back in sight."

* * *

Jessica was still blotting her neck.

"Say, Pete, would you make another phone call, please?" Jessica asked.

Pete dialed and, as she suspected, Jessica no longer felt the twinge in her neck; just the ache of the knife cut.

"Now, why did that chip react to the phone calls?" she wondered out loud.

Pete piped up with an explanation. "To put it in layman's terms, both the phone and the chip were transmitting using radio and sound waves. They just overlapped a little. like when your cell phone is sitting next to a computer, and you get some static on the screen just before the phone rings."

"They must have done it when I was knocked out. Well, all I can say is that I'm glad it's not in me anymore. Say, Pete, you seem to be a guy who is ready for just about anything. Do you have a Band-Aid in here somewhere?"

"Of course. I was a Boy Scout. I am always prepared," Pete said, producing one from his pocket.

Karl and Jessica exchanged amused glances.

"Hey, you never know," Pete said in defense. "And, if you don't mind, may I have my knife back now?"

* * *

"We should be right on top of them," the operative said into his cell phone.

Their vehicle was quickly approaching the location of the beeping transmitter.

"They should appear just as soon as we get around this truck."

The truck turned, and the blinking icon indicated their target also turned. They followed.

"Pass the truck."

As they advanced around it, they realized no hearse was in sight.

"Your destination is behind you. Turn around," the automated voice from their monitor directed.

"It's the truck," he said. "Turn around and cut it off."

The sedan made a U-turn at full speed, careening with screeching tires, and pulled in front of the truck, almost making it crash into their vehicle. The men jumped out, weapons ready, and stormed the truck. To their dismay, it was an elderly man in overalls.

"What in the Sam Hill do you think you're doing?" shouted the red-faced driver. "You're lucky I didn't just plow right into you, you son of a buck. Hey, where do you think you're going? You just can't do that and leave. Hey! Hey!"

"We've lost them," a dejected operative reported.

The phone was slammed down, and his contact swiped his arm across the desk, tossing everything on it to the ground. He kicked anything within leg's reach.

* * *

"We're here," Pete announced into the intercom.

* * *

Jessica looked up to see a brown tower. A flash of another similarly foreboding entrance crossed her mind. The light dimmed into darkness. She heard the rhythmic clanking of metal wheels slowly moving over railroad tracks. The stench of packed bodies and bodily excretions assaulted her senses. The railcar swayed to a stop with a sudden jerk, jostling everyone one last time. A loud clunk meant the door was being unlocked, which caused the inhabitants of this packed car to surge toward the entrance, desperate for fresh air.

As the door opened, the mass of humans hesitated as the blinding sunlight streamed into the blackness that had been their companion for days. A collective sharp inhalation, gasping to renew the senses as a blast of crisp air burst through the car.

She moved with the group, shuffling toward the light, almost too weak to move. Those able to move pressed hard behind her, reaching for the light, the nightmare of the trip finally over.

"Ah, sweet fragrance. This awful trip is over," a sweet elderly voice cackled in a language Jessica shouldn't have known.

"Fool," said another in the same foreign tongue. "If they cared so little for us to transport us like cattle, what makes you think their opinion of us cows will be better out of this box?"

"I don't care. I just want air and light."

Bickering and murmuring continued in hushed tones. Suddenly, she was out; the bright sun forced her eyes shut. Everyone was out of the railcar now except several bodies crumpled to one side. As she adjusted to the brightness, she continued to shuffle forward with the crowd.

Shielding her eyes, she looked up and saw the brown tower and the wrought iron gates with the words *Arbeit Macht Frei* (*Work Makes You Free*). Maybe there was hope; she was a good worker. Someone took her by the elbow.

* * *

"Here we are," she heard a familiar voice say. "Jessica, we're here."

Karl was lightly touching her elbow, as he guided her past the tower, into the entrance. Jessica shook her head, trying to clear the memories, and she realized she was back in the present.

"Where are we?" she asked.

"The National Holocaust Museum," Karl replied.

Jessica froze. "No."

Karl didn't understand. "This is where we're leaving the documents. It's fine to go in. In fact, I'd prefer we hurry up and get inside instead of being out here in plain sight."

"No. I'm sorry — I just... can't." Jessica couldn't explain it. She knew that stepping inside would be too much to bear. The combined grief and heartache that would flood over her would be overwhelming. Over the past few days, she had doubted many things, but this one thing she knew for sure: she was not going to cross that threshold.

Karl was at his wit's end. He didn't want to leave Jessica alone.

"Pete, stay here. I'll be right back." Karl hesitated a moment, squeezed Jessica's hand, and disappeared into the museum. Soon, Karl and the director returned to the hearse.

"Jessica, Pete, this is Mr. Robinowitz."

"Robino-what?" Pete asked.

"You've almost got it. Rob-in-o-witz. But, please, just call me

Arnold," he said, warmly shaking their hands. "Thank you so much for your efforts." He then addressed Jessica directly. "I am truly sorry you have had to suffer at their hands."

Jessica shook his hand and nodded.

Arnold continued, "These documents are the missing link that we've needed to return so many objects to their rightful owners." His voice cracked. In a more subdued tone, he said, "We have been praying for something like this to happen. I just couldn't imagine that it could be this…"

He trailed off, overcome with emotion. Arnold reached out and encompassed both of her hands in his in a heartfelt embrace. "Thank you." His eyes were glistening.

Jessica couldn't speak. Instead, she gave him a warm embrace, her eyes brimming over with tears.

Karl took a deep breath, sniffed loudly, then turned to Pete and gave him a slap on the shoulder. "Hey, thanks, man. Mr. Robin-o… Uh, Arnold here can tell you where to unload our cargo."

A car pulled up, startling Jessica.

"Jessica, this car is for us. No worries. They're the good guys," Karl assured her.

Shaking Arnold's hand, he said, "It's all in your hands now."

"Thank you. May God bless you both richly. Safe travels," Mr. Robinowitz said as the driver held open the car door for them to slide into the back seat.

They exchanged glances. Could this ordeal be coming to an end? Karl took Jessica's hand as they drove away in silence.

10

KANSAS CITY

The curator of the Nelson-Atkins Museum of Art met Karl and Jessica at the storage facility where they had stored the artwork. As Karl threw open the door, the curator gasped.

"Oh, heavens! I can't believe this."

His connections in Washington had only said to meet them as soon as possible. Now the secrecy to which he was bound became clear.

The museum's specially appointed moving truck backed up to the storage unit, and his team began their task of documenting and crating the treasure to prepare it for transport.

11

BRUSSELS

The elderly couple sat at the tiny table in their modest apartment. A knock at the door interrupted their breakfast. The old man shuffled over to the door laden with the multiple security locks appropriate for the neighborhood.

"Who is it?" his feeble voice cried out.

"I am Harry Johnston of the War Crimes Restitution Organization. I have some good news for you. May I come in?"

He laboriously unlocked the devices and slowly, suspiciously opened the door, giving the young man in the business suit a skeptical overview.

"Are you Abram Cohen?" Harry asked.

"And what if I were? All right, yes, I am," the grizzled old man replied.

"May I come in?"

Abram let Harry enter and pulled another stool over to the little kitchen table. Harry retrieved a packet of papers from his briefcase and began explaining why he was there. The couple held hands, tears streaming down their faces, the old, tattooed numbers peeking out from the edges of their sleeves, as they absorbed the news with disbelief. Their life would never be the same.

12

LONDON

The fifty-something woman exited the elevator onto her floor; cubicles as far as the eye could see.

"Good morning," she said, greeting her coworkers as part of her usual routine. Instead of the usual reply, they just looked up at her.

That's odd, she thought, then shrugged it off.

Then she noticed everyone staring at her. Was she in another one of her odd dreams that reeked of paranoia? No, but just as uncomfortable. Her typical fast stride slowed as she wondered what was going on. She finally approached her cubicle.

"Uh... there's someone here to see you," her supervisor said. "Come into my office."

Her boss led her into his glass-walled office space and held and shut the door for her, opting not to enter the office himself. The entire office watched as the two visitors explained to her about the lost wealth of her great grandparents, how it had now been reconnected to her family, and now being returned to her, the last living descendant of that line. Her initial reticence turned into disbelief. She sank against the desk with her hands over her mouth. Her life would never be the same.

13

BROOKLYN

The small group of mourners had gathered at the cemetery, paying their final respects to Magda, the matriarch of the Gutman family. No one noticed the two representatives from the War Crimes Restitution team hovering among the distant trees. As the group dispersed from the gravesite, the two approached Magda's next of kin.

"Mr. Gutman?" they asked the gentleman, whose face they recognized from their identity search.

"Yes. I'm sorry, I don't think we've met. How did you know my mother?" he asked, gathering his emotions.

"We've only met through her past, I regret to say. I'm sorry we didn't connect prior to her passing."

"Excuse me?" Mr. Gutman was confused.

They then summarized for him the restoration of the vast amounts of artwork that had been a part of the Gutman estate prior to World War II.

Mr. Gutman reached out to support himself against a nearby tree. "If only she had known."

14

CHICAGO

A well-groomed gentleman sat behind his massive desk in an enormous corner office lined with windows displaying Chicago's million-dollar view. He had been lost in thought when the intercom buzzed.

"Mr. Levine, there's someone here to see you. He says its important," his secretary relayed.

Howard Levine didn't come from a wealthy family; he didn't grow up with the amenities that he could well afford now. But he knew in the back of his mind how to live that kind of lifestyle in Warsaw, Poland. He was the youngest child of one of the most respected families in the area.

But Howard wasn't cut from the same cloth. Instead of the starched white clothes his parents preferred him to wear as a boy, he much preferred his play clothes, not fitting in with the elitist mentality. He was continually chastised for opting to play rough and tumble games with the servant's children, but in the end, it was his salvation.

That had been exactly what he was doing the day they came for his family. He watched through the latticework under the massive wraparound porch as they dragged his family out onto the grounds, then into the waiting vehicle, never to be seen again. As soon as he realized what was happening, he wanted to save his family, as hopeless as that was. His life was spared that day by the servant's son, who held him down with a hand clasped over his mouth to protect him from also being taken.

The servants took him under their wing and raised him as their own. They had loved their employers, who had been kind and generous to them, and were devastated that they were gone, and their magnificent home ransacked by the Nazis. As soon as was possible, they relocated to Pennsylvania and began a new life.

As an adult, he reverted to his given name to honor his family's heritage. Howard excelled at everything he attempted, becoming rich and successful. In time, he saw with gratitude all that his adoptive family and childhood friend had done for him, richly rewarding them for their unselfish love for him.

By the time the representatives from the Jewish Restitution Board finalized their business with Howard, he had already decided his plan of action.

"I don't need it," he told them to their surprise. "But I know of some place that does."

He instructed them to give all the proceeds to the Chicago Coalition for the Homeless, specifically earmarked for homeless children. It made him shudder to think what would have happened to him if someone hadn't accepted him into their own home when he lost his. He would make sure other children also rose above their circumstances. Their lives would never be the same.

15

KANSAS CITY

"How long will it take to sell?" Karl asked Jessica, loading the last box into the van.

Jessica rolled her eyes. "Well, if I had a crystal ball, I could tell you. Does next week sound good?" she snarked.

"Sure, sounds great," Karl replied.

"You're very funny. But seriously, Karl, there's a real solid buyer who is going to take a look at the house for a second time. Cash buyer, so you never know."

"Terrific." He grabbed her by the waist and swung her around. "Good riddance! Any of the good memories I had here as a boy soured once I found out who Grandpa really was."

He put her down and took her hands.

"Hey," Karl said in a more serious tone, "there's something else I wanted to show you."

Jessica cocked her head as Karl opened the car door for her, and she got in.

16

INDEPENDENCE

They drove about half an hour east of Kansas City on the interstate, took a midtown exit, and had been driving on a side street for a few minutes when Karl turned into a gated drive. He stopped and entered a security code, which made the gates slowly open.

"What's this?" Jessica asked.

"Evidently, Grandpa bought these forty acres a long time ago under a separate trust so it would pass to me without anyone's knowledge. Looks like all woods, right? Well, they used to quarry limestone from here. The whole place is laced with tunnels. In the safety deposit box, there was a map of them — about three million square feet of tunnels right under our feet," Karl said as the drive dipped, where they stopped in front of a garage door cut into the side of the rock wall.

Karl entered a second code into the keypad. The garage door slowly opened, and they entered the darkness. Lights automatically came on as they passed, and the garage door shut with a bang, cutting off any natural light.

"Solar panels," Karl said. "And motion detectors. Look behind us."

Jessica looked over the back seat to see the lights beginning to turn off as they moved forward. At the end of the parking garage, there was a door. They parked, and Karl entered a third code in the panel for the door to unlock.

"Are you ready?" Karl asked her.

"I'm not sure. Am I?" Jessica didn't know what to make of this.

Karl took her by the hand as he went down the long hallway, the hall lights also connected to motion sensors which turned off soon after they passed by.

"It's kind of cold in here," Jessica noted with a shiver.

Karl grinned. "These tunnels are like caves. Constantly about sixty-five degrees year-round. No heating, no cooling, no need. Great for storing stuff, and Kansas City is riddled with these tunnels. They were created for mining limestone, and that ended in this area in the 1950s."

Jessica nodded. "Interesting. I didn't know."

"Here we are," Karl said as they rounded a bend. He hesitated, then opened the door.

The light flickered on as the door opened, illuminating stacks of gold bars as far as they could see into the darkness.

Jessica gasped. "What the...?"

"You see, my grandfather never really did trust banks. Plus, he knew how to embezzle from those other Nazis who would give him grief over the years, and some of them headed up some pretty large corporations worth billions of dollars. And I don't really have a moral problem with keeping *their* money. Besides, what would they spend it on? Trying to take over the world?" Karl said with a wink.

"Wow." was all that Jessica could muster.

"Honey, we're rich." Karl grabbed her and spun her around. "Let's remember this day as the beginning of a new day. There's way more here than we'll ever need, so let's brainstorm as to how we can distribute a bit of this every year to someone who *really* needs it."

Jessica took Karl by the lapels of his coat and planted a big wet kiss on his lips. He reciprocated and their passion escalated. They tumbled onto one of the pallets of gold bars, not being able to, or wanting to, stop themselves. The dark comfort of the cave echoed with the sounds of their lovemaking, the gold bars reflecting the overhead lights, giving their skin a rich glow. Finally spent, both lay with their backs upon the gold, watching the flickering amber reflections dance on the rock hewn walls.

Suddenly, the lights went out. Jessica screamed. Karl laughed and moved his arms to reactivate the motion sensor, and the lights came back on.

Jessica tried to hit him. "That scared me."

Karl intercepted her fist and lovingly kissed it. "Let's get out of here."

He grabbed a couple of ingots, testing their weight in his hand. They retraced their steps to the exit, this time not having to enter codes. Sensors in the garage automatically opened the door and gates as they left.

Jessica's cell phone beeped that she had a message. "Funny, I didn't even hear it ring."

"Oh, I'm sure being underground can block the signal," Karl said, making a mental note for future reference.

Jessica listened to her voicemail with a quizzical look on her face. "They want to meet with me," she said.

"Who?"

"The reps at the Nelson-Atkins Museum. They want to see me right away," Jessica replied.

"Okay, we're done here. Let's go," Karl said, turning back towards downtown Kansas City.

* * *

"Well, Miss Sinclair, I'm happy you were able to meet with us so quickly," Mona Thomas, the director, said, shaking Jessica's hand and motioning toward a chair. "Please, sit down."

Jessica and Karl sat in the rich leather chairs offered to them.

"Now, Miss Sinclair, your grandfather was Daniel Sinclair?" she began.

"Yes…" Jessica said hesitantly, "he was at Terezin. He always said that God had watched over him because he got out alive — but for a price. He also said he was worth every penny."

"Did you know his name was in the ledgers?" Mona inquired.

"Well, actually, yes. I saw his name in the Terezin book and the one from his town. Why do you ask?" Jessica was getting more curious.

"His name is also in another book. Did you know that?" she asked.

"Why, no."

Mona continued, "Did you know that he once had a large estate in Austria?"

"Well, I've heard family stories. Well, some. The past was a subject not discussed very often. My grandparents had too many dark memories."

Mona repositioned herself directly in front of Jessica. "There were pieces of art and collectibles of your grandparents that were confiscated at the onset of the war."

"Oh?" Jessica wasn't expecting this.

"Yes, in fact..." She motioned to the other part of her office where a large painting rested on an easel, draped in a black cloth. Mona nodded, and her assistant pulled away the covering.

Jessica gasped. It was the Vermeer that had been over the fireplace mantle that had spoken to her.

* * *

"Hey, Granny," Jessica said in a hushed tone as she entered the room at the nursing home. "I have something for you."

Jessica went back out into the hallway and brought in the painting, setting it on her dresser.

"This was Grandpa's. It's yours now."

Her grandmother's glistening eyes met Jessica's, then moved to gaze at the painting. She just rocked back and forth in her chair as Jessica sat, holding her delicate little hand, watching her glowing face, tears streaming down her cheeks. After sitting with her granny for a while, Jessica leaned over, kissed her cheek, and said goodbye. Jessica turned at the doorway and looked at her one last time, a small smile on her face.

Lorene continued to rock slowly, staring at the painting, welcoming the flood of peace that engulfed her. She somehow knew that the haunting visions that had plagued her for a lifetime were put to rest. A huge wave of relief overcame her as a single tear worked its way down her cheek. Her tissue-paper thin skin tightening as her hand tensed for a moment before slowly sliding down the arm of her chair as she finally joined the rest of her family, who had been patiently watching over her for so many years.

* * *

The polished perfect gentleman signed the final documents and was handed the keys.

"Congratulations. It's all yours. It's an awesome place. I hope you enjoy it. Do you have a large family?" the officiate at the title company asked, reaching over to shake his hand.

"Yes, well, something like that..." the new homeowner replied, receiving her hand in his, revealing a signet ring with a familiar crest on his right hand.

THE END

ABOUT THE AUTHOR

Heidi Bacon is an American novelist who uses her experience as a former Realtor, artist, filmmaker, and researcher and draws on her family history to weave historical fiction stories. When not writing, Heidi likes to paint, teach art classes and oversee The Artist Sanctuary, an arts nonprofit organization that she founded and is Executive Director. Heidi was born and raised in the Midwest and spent a decade in Savannah, GA, where she married and started a family. Three children later, after raising alpacas & other animals in Colorado, having art galleries, and a divorce in Kansas, Heidi and her children relocated to Minnesota, where previous generations of her family had settled. Heidi and her sisters created plays and stories as children, and expressed their creativity through Children's Theater, Children's Orchestra, ballet, violin, and piano lessons. As an adult,

Heidi has been a Master Naturalist volunteer, worked in the Department of Commerce, Department of Health, and Department of Agriculture, and created murals for Minnesota's State Parks. Her interest in history, archaeology, genealogy, caving, and cryptozoology inspired her stories.

AFTERWORD

Go to hangarıpublishing.com to learn more about the Authors and stay up to date with their newest releases.

Printed in the USA
CPSIA information can be obtained
at www.ICGtesting.com
JSHW011916141024
71676JS00011B/43